Anita Prichard's Complete
CANDY COOKBOOK

Anita Prichard's Complete CANDY COOKBOOK

By Anita Prichard
Photographs by Martin Jackson

H·A·R·M·O·N·Y B·O·O·K·S

New York

In memory of Anne Udin, Higbee's book buyer "extraordinary" who inspired the writing of the book, and to my sister, Win, who helped develop and test the recipes.

Let me also express my special thanks to the elderly ladies in Fairmount, Illinois who laboriously copied their time-tested recipes as their contribution in reviving a lost art.

My appreciation, in abundance, goes to two young editors, Linda Sunshine and Marcy Posner, for their painstaking efforts in editing the manuscript. I add my thanks to Janet Sutherland, who designed the book and to Mary Barnwell for helping to prepare the creative packaging for photographing.

Harmony Books
a division of Crown Publishers, Inc.
One Park Avenue, New York, New York 10016

Book and cover design: Janet Sutherland

Candy dishes on the cover courtesy of Lord & Taylor.

Published simultaneously in Canada by General Publishing Co., Ltd. Printed in the United States of America.

Library of Congress Cataloging in Publication Data

Prichard, Anita.
  Anita Prichard's Complete candy cookbook.

  1. Confectionery. I. Title. II. Title: Complete candy cookbook.
TX791.P89 1978   641.8'53   78-15616
ISBN 0-517-53245-X

CONTENTS

INTRODUCTION

At a time when everyone is food-preservative-conscious homemade candy is back in style! Making candy has become a new food fashion. Department stores and specialty shops feature candy boutiques that sell confections made with natural ingredients. A creatively packaged box of hand-dipped chocolates is the perfect gift for any occasion.

Perhaps the craft age we live in contributes to the rise of interest in candy-making. Such interest is not necessarily tied to economic problems. "For some reason, people continue to eat candies whatever the economic situation," as one prominent candy manufacturer pointed out.

Rather, it may be in part the call of nostalgia. More and more of us are returning to simple home satisfactions, like making by hand, in the old-fashioned way, attractive and delicious sweets for the pleasure of those we love.

Home candy-making has been an integral aspect of family life in America from the late eighteenth century on through the days of the depression when taffy pulls and fudge-making parties were a natural part of growing up.

Prosperity and possibly World War II put an end to such amusements. As the wheels of the country began to turn increasingly fast, there was little time, and little need, to make one's own candy. Fudge mixes and chocolate bits could be picked up from supermarket shelves. Manufacturers, using new techniques and new machinery, could spin out all kinds of assembly-line candy. They might not have quite the same flavor as the candies your grandmother made; nevertheless, a nickel in a machine gave you a chocolate-covered, nut-filled candy bar as fast as your hand could catch it.

From the 30's on, in fact, old-fashioned candy recipes gradually disappeared from cookbooks. One authority on American cooking attributes the entire demise of home candy-making as a popular form of cooking to the casual recording of the old recipes. Early cookbooks gave almost no space to candy-making instructions; it was assumed that every cook, even a young bride, knew how to make candy.

Suddenly, in the 70's, both the art and the recipes have come back to life.

For this book, I became a recipe detective. The women in my family have always been home candymakers and I hunted down family diaries and journals—some of them more than a hundred years old—from which I culled candy recipes that appeared among notes about births, deaths, bad weather, good harvests, and how to cure hams. The recipes were actually lists of ingredients (without measurements), and such instructions as "Stir a while" I translated into modern culinary language.

I also wrote down for the first time family candy recipes that have been handed down from mother to daughter for generations. I enlisted my sister in the chase. She, in turn, enlisted the help of her friends and co-workers. Everyone got caught up in the spirit of recipe hunting and uncovered many marvelous recipes from the past.

Once they were gathered, the important task of testing began. Recipes in any cookbook must be checked by actual cooking, and for candy this is particularly vital. Almost all the luscious cooked candies in the world contain just four basic ingredients: sugar, liquid, butterfat, and flavoring. It is the range of cooking temperatures that changes the ingredients, the sugar particularly, into so many varieties of candy. With the possible exception of refined French sauces, the cooking of no other food depends so exclusively on the nuances of temperature control.

The recipes in this book were tested meticulously by experts under the same sort of conditions that confront a candy cook at home. Among the junior cooks were my nieces and their high school friends, who became my teen-age authorities. They tested recipes in after-school candy-making sessions. My panel of tasters was made up of friends and fellow candy cooks, people like you and the members of your family who will be enjoying the candy you make.

Through this comprehensive collection of recipes—which runs from pioneer *Cream Candy* to a revolutionary easy method for dipping chocolates—you are invited to take the nicest possible step back in time and discover for the 1970's the great fun of making candy at home.

Candy-Making: A Short History

When the Greek gods on Olympus sat down to dine on ambrosia, it is possible that what they actually ate was a sweet candy brittle made of honey. The mystery of just what ambrosia really was is hidden in the Olympian clouds, but mythology tells us that, in addition to being an aid to immortality, it was "nine times as sweet as honey," which aptly describes honey boiled down to a brittle.

Cavemen were probably the first humans to imitate the gods and feast on candy. Our sweet tooth is surely a heritage from way back then. Cavemen had honey available in nearby trees and they used fire. Boiling the one over the other—perhaps accidentally the first time—very likely produced that delightful addition to a diet that has been with us ever since. We might even call cavemen and women the original home candy-makers.

Historically, however, the first to make candy were the ancient Egyptians, who mixed honey with fruits and spices. These became the kind of sweets we now define as confections.

Candy began to be made from sugar around the eleventh century, after Arabs learned how to process sugar and exported their discovery to the rest of the civilized world of that time. In fact, the Arabs gave us our English word for sweets. When fourteenth-century Crusaders came back to England from the Holy Lands, they used the word "quand" for what people at home called "sweetmeats." "Quand" quickly became "candy" and part of the English language, although it never completely replaced the original Anglo-Saxon term. Most of my English friends today still refer to candy as sweetmeats.

In the Middle Ages in Europe candy-making was the exclusive province of apothecaries, who no doubt combined their talents to invent sugarcoated pills!

When America began, apothecaries controlled candy-making in the New World too. Credit for introducing sugarcane to the Americas goes to Columbus. He is supposed to have brought it to San Domingo on the second of his four voyages, and from there it went north in the trade of Caribbean sugar for tobacco from the Colonies. Colonial housewives apparently used sugar for tea and cakes but not for candy.

It was not until the great westward movement of the nineteenth century that apothecaries lost their candy-making monopoly and American women began to make their own. The history of my own family traces this change. Both of my grandmothers were expert storytellers, and I grew up listening to accounts of the lives of *their* grandparents who, as part of that migration, went from Virginia, through the Cumberland Gap into east Tennessee, and on past Kentucky to settle finally in the new state of Indiana. In the wilderness of the frontier, these hardy ancestors of mine, many gently bred, depended on raw ingenuity to survive. Almost everything had to come from the land. It took a horse and rider the better part of a week to make the round trip to and from the nearest trading post for the few absolute necessities the farm could not provide. The women had the responsibility of turning farm produce into food that would not only sustain but would also sweeten the difficult life.

Many of the women kept careful journals of their daily activities. In those journals are recipes and among them is the first proof I have been able to find of candy made at home. Frontier women at their hearths boiled up maple sugar, honey, dried fruits, nuts, sorghum, and other home-grown ingredients into assortments of primitive confections.

The Victorian Age marked the high point of fancifulness in candy-making and recipes were complicated. Victorian cooks were using such ingredients as bourbon and the richest possible chocolate to make Kentucky Colonels, for instance, a fondant rich with bourbon, thick with chocolate.

A personal note: One of my storytelling grandmothers, my Grandmother Heavin, was expert at many elaborate recipes. One of my earliest memories is of sampling her annual groaning board of Christmas candies. She was, however, a complete Puritan, who believed that man was put on Earth to improve himself, not to amuse himself. She was also thrifty. Despite a household of nine children, she made not one candy for fifty-one weeks of the year. In the fifty-second week, she relented. For seven days during the Christmas season, my mother and her sisters and brothers enjoyed all the candy they could eat.

We have hilarious family stories about this annual one-week indulgence—which, incidentally, left all nine children with an insatiable craving for candy that they never outgrew. My mother, however, felt so deprived of sweets when she was young that she made candy of all sorts for her own five children whenever they asked. Is it much of a surprise that I am a home candymaker too?

The recipes in this book include many that are basically my mother's from the start of the twentieth century, versions of *her* mother's candies a generation earlier, fantasies from the Victorian era, adaptations of the recipes of frontier women, sweets related to the original Mideast confections—and included as well is honey brittle, the ambrosia of the gods.

CANDY
KNOW-HOW

Equipment

Equipment Needed for the Beginner:

(Essential) The following simple utensils:

1. Saucepans—1-, 2-, and 3-quart (1-, 2-, and 3-liter)—are most frequently used for recipes in this book. A heavy metal pan is a must for making cooked candies. It holds a uniform heat, and the candy does not stick readily or scorch while cooking.

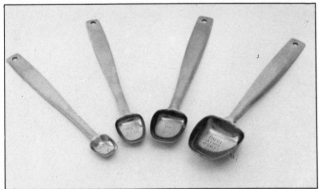

2. Set of measuring spoons.

3. Set of measuring cups, in graduated sizes of ¼, ⅓, ½, and 1 cup (60, 80, 120, and 240 ml).

4. Wooden mixing spoons.

5. Knives.

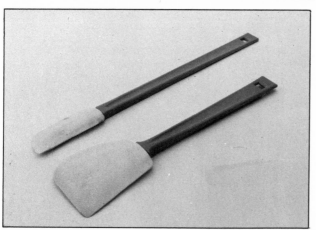

6. Rubber spatulas.

7. Scissors.

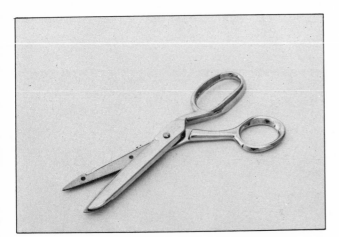

8. Candy spatulas; used for creaming candy on a baking sheet. These are actually paint scrapers with 3-inch to 5-inch stiff blades and can be bought in paint and hardware stores.

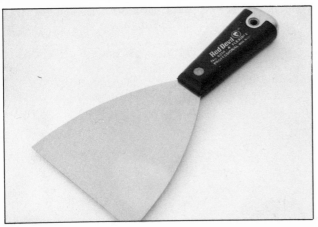

9. Shallow pans in sizes 8 x 8 x 2 inches, 9 x 9 inches.

10. Shallow pan 9 x 12 inches.

11. Baking sheet approximately 11 x 17 inches.

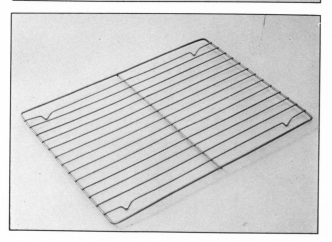

12. Wire rack to place under baking sheet for rapid cooling.

13. Containers to store candy. Two-pound (909-gram) coffee tins are ideal.

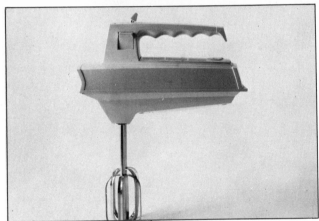

14. Electric hand mixer.

15. 1-quart (1-liter) double boiler.

16. Wooden cutting board.

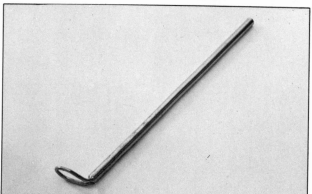

17. Dipping fork for coating bon-bons and caramels. See p. 26 for making your own dipping fork in a pinch.

18. Wire sifter.

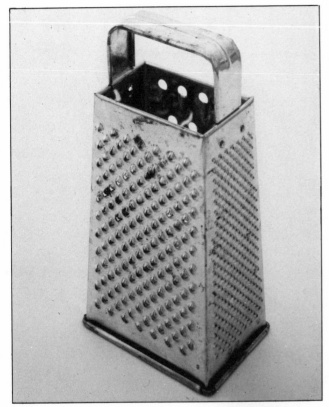

19. Hand grater for grating chocolate.

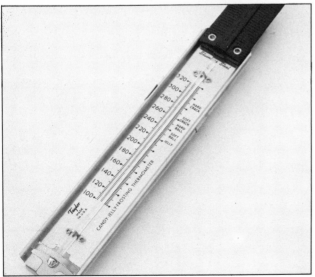

20. Candy thermometer; used to test accurately the temperature of candy syrup.

Advanced Equipment

You may want to add the following equipment as you progress in the craft of candy-making:

1. Blender or food processor; these modern, multi-speed kitchen aids take care of all the tedious chopping of nuts and fruits, easily and in seconds.

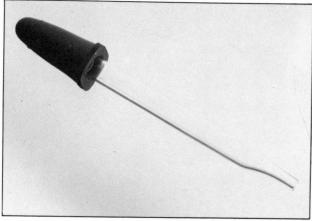

2. Medicine dropper; for accurately measuring oils and flavorings in recipes specifying "a few drops."

3. Oster Foodcrafter for quick grating of chocolate.

4. Candy cutting wheel. Sold by confectioners' supply houses (or use a pizza cutter).

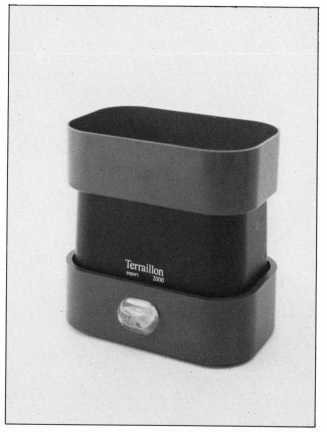

5. Kitchen scales.

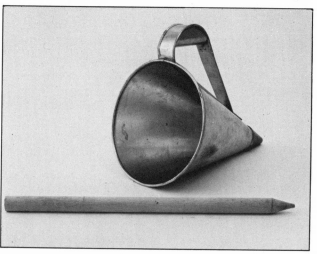

6. Funnel and stick; used to make mint patties. Sold by confectioners' supply houses.

The Indispensable Candy Thermometer:

Accurate cooking temperature is essential at almost every stage of candy-making and your best tool for the job is a candy thermometer.

Veteran candymakers can tell when candy is "done" by its appearance alone or by its "feel" in the cold-water test. But the acquisition of such skill takes years of experience as well as constant practice. Amateurs are ardently advised to rely on the thermometer.

Types of Candy Thermometers. I recommend clearly marked, easy-to-read, accurate thermometers with mercury bulbs that are set low enough to measure the heat in the boiling syrup but that do not touch the bottom of the pan—and with clips to hold them inside of the pan while in use. Several such thermometers are available; my personal preference is for the Taylor Candy Thermometer.

Candy Thermometer For Home Use. Temperature range of 100°F. (38°C.) to 320°F. (160°C.) is suitable for everything from *Easy-Method Chocolate Dipping* to hard candies, as well as for such non-candies as jellies and frostings. The thermometer comes with instructions and a temperature chart on the back of an attached card. (See Sources of Supply, p. 217.)

Commercial Candy Thermometer. If you make candy in large quantities for profit or benefits and bazaars, you won't be satisfied with anything but the commercial version by Taylor. Its cost is approximately twice that of the smaller thermometer, but it is stainless steel, and the scale is large and easy to read. This thermometer is not meant for use with small saucepans, as it is 12 inches long, and the weight of the handle could cause a small pan to topple over. The temperature range is from 60°F. (16°C.) to 360°F. (182°C.)

To Test Candy Thermometer: Test a candy thermometer for accuracy by putting it in a pan of cold water with mercury bulb completely submerged. Bring water to boil and let boil for several minutes. The thermometer should register 212°F. (100°C.), at sea level and 1 degree less for approximately every thousand feet above sea level.

High-Altitude Testing Of Candy Thermometer. If the temperature at boiling point is below 212°F. (100°C.), subtract the number of degrees below this mark from the cooking temperature in the recipe.

The following table gives temperatures for altitudes of four thousand feet or more:

Soft-Ball Stage	218-228°F.
	103-109°C.
Firm-Ball Stage	232-240°F.
	111-116°C.
Hard-Ball Stage	250-260°F.
	121-127°C.
Soft-Crack Stage	260-270°F.
	127-132°C.
Hard-Crack Stage	275-280°F.
	135-138°C.
Caramelized Sugar	286-290°F.
	141-143°C.

To Use Candy Thermometer: Be sure the thermometer is at room temperature before inserting it into hot syrup. Lower thermometer gradually into candy mixture *after* sugar is dissolved and boiling has started. Be sure the bulb of thermometer is immersed in the syrup, but be careful to keep it from touching bottom of the pan. (With the Taylor thermometers the bulb is high up.) When finished with the thermometer, remove it from the hot syrup and immerse it in hot water. This will make the delicate instrument easier to clean later.

To Read Candy Thermometer, keep it in upright position with mercury bulb completely under boiling syrup. This is one reason for using the correct-sized pan as specified in the recipe. Eye should be level with top of mercury for an accurate reading. Reading the thermometer on a slanted angle may mean one or two degrees above or below the cooking temperature, and this makes a difference in the finished product.

To Clean Candy Thermometer, use warm, sudsy water. Check carefully to make sure you have removed all sugar crystals. Any crystals left on the thermometer will haunt your next candy-making attempt.

Improvising in a Pinch

How to Test Without a Candy Thermometer: If you are not supplied with a thermometer, use the following procedure: First, remove the candy from heat. The mixture can change rapidly from one stage to another if it continues to cook while you are testing. Drop a little cooked syrup—about ¼ teaspoon (1.25 ml)—into 1 cup (240 ml) of cold but not ice water and quickly pinch the ball between the thumb and finger. The following are the cold-water stages.

Soft-Ball Stage (for fondant, fudges, and penuches) the syrup forms a soft ball which flattens out between fingers.

Firm-Ball Stage (for caramels, nougat, and divinities) the syrup forms a stiff ball which retains its shape for a minute or two when held between the fingers.

Hard-Ball Stage (for molasses, taffy, and soft candies to be pulled) the syrup forms a hard ball that will roll about on a buttered surface when removed from the water.

Soft-Crack Stage (for toffee, butterscotch, crunches, and hard candies) the syrup forms spirals or threads that are brittle under water

but which soften and become sticky when removed from the water.

Hard-Crack Stage (for clear brittle candies, glacé, and some hard candies) the syrup forms spirals or threads that are brittle when removed from the water and do not stick to the fingers.

Caramelized Sugar No cold-water test. Sugar liquifies and caramelizes to light toast shade. Do not overcook or the sugar will burn.

How to Make a Dipping Fork: This is not really a fork but a metal loop fastened at almost a right angle to a long handle or make your own as follows (see Sources of Supply, p. 217):

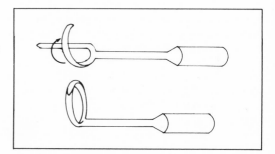

1. Use a straight length of copper wire about 10 inches long and heavy enough to shape and bend (coat-hanger wire is too heavy). Make a loop 1½ inches from the end of the wire. Twist the ends tightly to form a circle about ½ inch in diameter; bend at right angle to form handle. Do not make the loop too large or your coated centers will slip through it and fall back into the pan.

2. Alternatively, you can make a dipping fork from an inexpensive two-pronged roasting fork. With pliers, gently bend each prong about 1 inch from the end at right angles to the handle of the fork. This homemade dipper works very well for handling large centers and for caramel dipping.

Ingredients and How to Use Them:

Accurate measuring can make the difference between success and failure. If you're a brand-new candy cook, the following rules will help you start off right.

When Your Recipe Calls for Sugar:

Granulated is the sugar generally used in candy-making. Granulated and Extra Fine Granulated can be used interchangeably in the recipes in this book. *Superfine* is a very fine quick-dissolving granulated sugar. Use Superfine in areas of high humidity to help retard excessive crystallization in the making of cream and hard candies.

Always sift granulated sugar before measuring to remove large grains which will be difficult to dissolve. Sift it onto waxed paper, spoon it into the measuring cup, then level off with a spatula.

Confectioners' Sugar is granulated sugar crushed very fine and mixed with cornstarch to prevent caking. Do *not* substitute this sugar for Granulated in candy recipes. Sift and measure as for Granulated.

Light and Dark Brown Sugars are essentially the same, but the light brown has a milder flavor and is used more often for candy. Because brown sugar has a rather high acid content, it usually makes milk or cream curdle at the boiling point. But you need the acidity to produce a creamy candy, so don't worry about the curdling. It will disappear during the final beating.

Spoon brown sugar into the measuring cup a little at a time. Pack it down firmly with the back of the spoon. When turned out, it should stand up as if molded.

When Your Recipe Calls for Cream of Tartar or Baking Soda:

Cream of Tartar is used in some recipes to give the candy a creamier consistency.

Baking Soda combines with the acids in such candy ingredients as honey and brown sugar to produce a gas that makes brittles and crunches separate into layers. Honeycomb Brittle is a perfect example of this chemical process.

Measure both of the above ingredients very carefully; too much of either one will give flavor to the candy and make it heavy and difficult to cream in the final beating.

When Your Recipe Calls for Liquids:

Glass measures with a spout and a slight edge above the top marking are musts, and you'll find 1-, 2-, and 4-cup (240, 480, and 960 ml) sizes a boon to saving time. When measuring, place the cup on a flat surface so you can read it at an even level.

Corn Syrup is used extensively in candy-making. Professionals call it glucose. Do not substitute dark corn syrup when the recipe calls for light. The use of corn syrup tends to prevent grainy candy.

Molasses and Sorghum can be used interchangeably in the recipes in this book.

Honey called for in the recipes in this book is the liquid type sold in grocery stores and nutrition centers.

Whipping Cream is known as heavy cream in some localities and is about 35 to 40 percent butterfat. This produces the richest candy.

Undiluted Evaporated Milk can be substituted for whipping cream.

Light Cream, or coffee cream, contains 18 to 20 percent butterfat and produces a candy slightly less rich than whipping cream does.

Use Whole Milk, not skimmed, in any recipe that calls for milk. Skimmed milk does not contain enough butterfat.

Dried Skimmed Milk Solids mixed with water can replace milk in recipes if you add 2 tablespoons (30 ml) of butter.

Dried Creams, which are milk solids plus light cream solids, have varying butterfat contents. Check the label.

Diluted Evaporated Milk (half and half) is a legitimate substitute for milk in candy recipes.

When Your Recipe Calls for Nuts:

To Store or Freeze Nuts. Light, heat, moisture, and exposure to air are factors which tend to make shelled nuts rancid. So the best way to store nuts is to leave them in their shells and place them in airtight plastic bags in a cool place or in the freezer. Shell difficult nuts, like pecans and Brazil nuts, before they thaw completely. Be sure to discard any kernels that are shriveled or dry; they will impart a bitter or rancid taste to candy. Shelled nuts may be kept from 2 months at about 70°F. (17°C.) to as long as 2 years if kept in the freezer.

The yield from whole nuts will average about 1 cup (240 ml) of nutmeats to a pound (454 grams).

To Blanch Nuts. Some shelled nuts have a thin inner lining of skin. If the recipe calls for blanched nutmeats, pour boiling water over the shelled nuts and let them stand for 1 minute at the most. Longer soaking will waterlog the kernels. Drain the nuts and pinch off the skins. Spread the nuts on a baking sheet to dry.

Alternate Method: For peanuts, filberts, and pistachio nuts, you may roast at 350°F. (177°C.) for about 15 minutes, then wrap the nuts in a tea towel while they are still warm and rub them around in the towel until friction loosens the skins.

To Roast Nuts. Most nuts, except pecans and walnuts, improve the taste of candy if they are first very lightly roasted to bring out their rich flavor. When roasting, leave the nuts in the largest possible pieces. Unless otherwise specified in a recipe, place the nuts— blanched or unblanched—in a 300°F. (149°C.) oven and turn frequently with a wooden spoon to avoid scorching. Remember, when roasted nuts are added to brittles, crunches, and toffees, the high temperature of the cooked syrup will continue to roast the nuts.

Alternate Method: My sister discovered this when one of my nieces burned a whole baking sheet of expensive almonds. The secret is perfect oven-temperature control. Preheat oven to 350°F. (177°C.) Place nuts in oven and immediately turn off the heat. Set timer for 15 minutes. Do not peek. Remove from oven immediately. Your nuts will be very lightly roasted and perfect for candy-making.

To Chop Nuts. Always chop nuts after they have been roasted. Use a chef's knife, hand grater, blender, or food processor.

To Prepare Fresh Coconut. It is a bother to prepare fresh coconut for candy-making, but every bit of effort pays off in delicious flavor. Start with an unopened coconut full of liquid. Pierce eyes with screwdriver. Drain off liquid; heat coconut in 350°F. (177°C.) oven for 15 to 30 minutes, or until coconut is cracked. Tap all over with hammer, then break open. Pry out meat and pare off dark skin. To grate meat, use grater, blender, or food processor.

To Toast Coconut. Spread grated coconut on baking sheet. Bake in 350°F. (177°C.) for about 15 minutes until light brown, stirring frequently.

To Tint Coconut. Mix a few drops of food coloring with a few drops of water in glass jar. Add approximately 1 cup grated coconut and shake until evenly colored.

To Freeze Coconut. Grate coconut. Pack into containers, allowing 1-inch space at the top for expansion.

Before You Begin:

Remember! The crystallizing of sugar into candy is a precision craft. A successful batch of candy depends upon meticulously following a recipe and carefully measuring ingredients. Do not substitute basic ingredients or alter quantities. To double a yield, make the recipe twice, do not double ingredients unless specified.

First Steps:

Step 1: Read through the *entire* recipe.

Step 2: Assemble all the equipment you need before you measure your ingredients. Adequate pan size is important in order to prevent boil-overs. Allow 1 quart (1 liter) of space for 1 cup (240 ml) of sugar. For example, if a recipe specifies 2 cups (480 ml) of sugar, use a 2-quart (2-liter) saucepan.

Step 3: Assemble and measure all ingredients. (See Ingredients and How to Use Them on page 27.)

Things to Know About Making Candy:

The Four Causes of Most Candy Failures.
Over-crystallization, inadequate measuring of ingredients, high humidity, and falling barometric pressure.

To Prevent Crystallization, sift all granulated sugar. Sugar absorbs the moisture from high humidity, so always sift any sugar, particularly if it has been standing for a length of time. Always wipe crystals from sides of saucepan before inserting the candy thermometer, or before the syrup comes to a second boil. Avoid any jarring or unnecessary movement of the syrup at a temperature above 110°F. (43°C.)

To Insure Accurate Measurements, double check the measurement marks on plastic cups and spoons against a pharmacist's medicine cup. You will find one at your friendly local drugstore.

To Combat High Humidity and Low Barometric Pressure. You can't! A humid day is the day to make candies from the *Quick and Easy* section (pp. 33-74) of this book and firm them in the refrigerator. Remember, cooked candy syrup will not cream properly unless the barometer is within the normal range or above. This applies whether or not it is raining. Local radio and TV stations usually give regular barometric reports. If yours doesn't, buy an inexpensive kitchen barometer.

Cooking Procedures:

1. Mix ingredients thoroughly before placing your pan over heat.

2. When you start to cook, stir all candy mixtures (unless recipe says otherwise) over moderate heat until the sugar dissolves and before boiling begins. Stirring helps keep sugar crystals from sticking together in the bottom of the pan, and the heat will dissolve them. Stir slowly and carefully to splash as little as possible on the sides of the pan. Splashing creates instant crystals. Before you insert your candy thermometer, wipe off the crystals that may have formed on the sides of the pan despite your care.

3. Cover all sugar and water mixtures for the first 2 or 3 minutes of boiling to soften the sugar crystals on the sides of the pan. Uncover and wipe crystals from the sides of the pan with a damp paper towel or small sponge.

4. Do not cover candy mixtures using milk products or molasses while cooking. They foam if steam cannot escape and may boil over.

5. Boil sugar and water mixtures over moderate heat. Cook cream or milk mixtures more slowly. Lower temperatures keep the syrup from scorching on the bottom of the pan. Watch closely near the end of the cooking period when the syrup thickens.

6. Remove cooking mixture immediately from the heat as soon as cooking temperature is reached. Even a few extra seconds can overcook candy.

7. For candies that need high temperature, cook very slowly for the last few degrees; the thermometer will go up faster than you expect.

8. Unless stated in recipe, do not scrape candy from pan when pouring. Scraping will cause it to crystallize.

9. When the humidity is only slightly marginal, cook candy 1 or 2 degrees higher than directed, as the candy will absorb moisture from the air while cooling. This trick will not work if you are having a prolonged period of rain.

10. If candy becomes too hard to spread, knead it like bread dough, then shape as desired. This actually improves the texture.

11. Baking sheets should either be dampened or lightly greased for use. In the latter case use the lightest possible vegetable oil or butter. Candy is porous and any other shortening will permeate and change the taste of the finished product.

Food Colorings and Flavorings:

Colorings. Food colors come in three forms—liquid, powder, and paste. Liquid colors are found in supermarkets, and are generally satisfactory for candy-making because the shades will remain pastel. However, if a brilliant shade is desired (as for making hard candies and marzipan), it is necessary to use paste or powder colors. (See Sources of Supply, p. 217.) All of these shades are available ready mixed, or you can make them at home by various blendings of the four basic colors.

Liquid coloring is measured by drops from the bottle; paste and powder colorings are measured in "toothpick" quantities—that is, the amount that will cling to the tip of a toothpick.

Color Blending Chart:

Color	Number of Drops			
	Red	*Yellow*	*Green*	*Blue*
Orange	1	3	—	—
Rust	3	3	—	—
Lavender	1	—	—	2
Purple	3	—	—	1
Olive Green	—	—	3	2
Lime	—	6	1	—
Chocolate Brown	3	2	2	—
Raspberry	8	—	—	1
Strawberry	7	1	—	—

Flavorings. A wide range of pure flavoring extracts and oils is available to you. (See Sources of Supply, p. 217.) Generally speaking, ¼ teaspoon (1.25 ml) of oil is equivalent to 1 teaspoon (5 ml) of flavoring extract.

Use flavoring oil if you want a strong concentrated flavor—in such candies as fondant, marzipan, and hard candies, for example.

Coloring And Flavoring Chart:

Flavor	Color
Anise	Pink
Apricot	Pale Orange
Banana	Yellow
Black Walnut	Light Brown
Butter Rum	Yellow Brown
Butterscotch	Yellow
Cherry	Red
Cinnamon	Red
Clove	Gold or Red
Coconut	White
Lemon	Yellow
Licorice	Black
Lime	Yellow Green
Maple	Pale Brown
Orange	Orange
Peppermint	Pink or White
Pineapple	Light Yellow
Raspberry	Blue Red
Spearmint	Green
Wintergreen	Pale Green or Pale Pink

QUICK AND EASY CANDY

Little cooking, no temperature testing with a thermometer, just measure and mix. This chapter will provide the candymaker with an imaginative selection of delicious confections. What could be more elegant than an assortment of Chocolate Truffles, Creamy Fudge, Bourbon Balls, Marshmallows, Jelly Candies, and Dried-Fruit Confections? Grand enough to stand alone in their simplicity, they may be further enhanced with a robe of Chocolate, Summer, Bonbon, or Caramel Coating. Each recipe gives detailed instructions for preparing coated and uncoated centers.

Because the crystallization of sugar is not involved in the making of these quick and easy confections, rainy and humid weather will not affect the results.

The keeping qualities of quick and easy confections have proved to be comparable to similar varieties that are cooked by crystallizing sugar. I often stockpile a variety of these confections to use as dipping centers and freeze them in airtight containers.

Chapter 1
QUICK AND EASY FUDGE

My editors often call upon me to make an attractive array of confections for tastings and photography. Invariably, these requests are made during a long rainy spell when we are practically afloat here in central New Jersey.

I find myself relying more and more on the versatility of the fudge recipes in this section. Not only are they mouth-meltingly good, but the marshmallow or cream cheese gives them good keeping qualities as well.

Basic Five-Minute Fudge

(Recommended as Centers for Chocolate, Summer, or Caramel Coating)

This recipe has appeared in cookbooks as Fantastic Fudge, Rainy-Day Fudge, Million-Dollar Fudge, and Mamie's Fudge. Around our family kitchen it is often the recipe selected by the teen-age cooks.

Under any name, it is a foolproof fudge that turns out right in any kind of weather. It becomes a colorful Christmas fudge when you use lightly roasted pistachio nuts and candied cherries.

Utensils:

1   2-quart heavy saucepan
1   set measuring cups
1   wooden spoon
1   square pan, 8 x 8 x 2 inches, lined with buttered foil

Ingredients:

1²⁄₃ cups (400 ml) granulated sugar
²⁄₃ cup (160 ml) (1 small can) evaporated milk, undiluted
1   package (6 ounces or 170 grams) semi-sweet chocolate bits
1½ cups (360 ml) miniature marshmallows
½ cup (120 ml) lightly roasted nuts (any kind), chopped
½ cup (120 ml) candied cherries, quartered (optional)

Preparation:

1. Combine sugar and milk in saucepan and cook over medium heat, stirring constantly with wooden spoon, until sugar is dissolved and mixture comes to a boil.

2. Boil, stirring continuously, for 5 minutes.

3. Remove from heat and quickly blend in chocolate bits and marshmallows with wooden spoon.

4. Add nuts and cherries.

5. Stir until thick; pour into pan lined with buttered foil.

6. Cool until firm.

7. Turn out onto smooth surface and cut in 1-inch squares.

This candy has very good keeping qualities, can be made in quantity, and is a very good traveling confection. It can be frozen in an airtight container up to 6 months.

Yield: 1¼ pounds (568 grams).

Variations:

This basic recipe lends itself to almost any variation as long as you do not substitute for the candy bits or marshmallows. I like to use glacé apricots and coconut. Chopped dates are also nice.

Continental Fudge: Omit nuts and substitute flaked coconut. Omit cherries and substitute glacé apricots, finely chopped.

Coconut Fudge: Omit the nuts and cherries. Substitute 1 cup (240 ml) lightly toasted coconut.

Penuche Fudge: Omit chocolate bits. Substitute butterscotch bits. Use 1 cup (240 ml) chopped walnuts or pecans and omit candied cherries. Add 1 teaspoon (5 ml) butterscotch flavoring, if desired.

Chocolate Mint Fudge: Use mint-flavored chocolate bits. Remove candy from heat and add 1 teaspoon (5 ml) peppermint extract or few drops of oil of peppermint. Use 1 cup (240 ml) chopped nuts and omit cherries.

Maple Fudge: Omit the chocolate bits. Substitute butterscotch bits. Remove from heat and stir in 1 teaspoon (5 ml) maple-flavored extract. Use 1 cup (240 ml) chopped walnuts or pecans. Omit candied cherries.

Layered Fudge: Choose two of the above variations. Pour first batch evenly into two 8 x 8 x 2-inch square pans. Prepare second batch and pour it evenly over the first batch. Cool until firm. Remove candy from pans as for Basic Recipe.

Chocolate "Philly" Fudge

(Recommended as Centers for Chocolate or Summer Coating)

Nan Wiley, a popular food columnist, says, "All the cream cheese fudges get asked for every holiday time because they are so easy, creamy and dependable. No cooking, no testing, no beating." This candy will stay moist for about 2 weeks.

Utensils:

1   large mixing bowl
1   set measuring spoons
1   set measuring cups
1   wooden spoon
1   square pan, 8 x 8 x 2 inches, lined with buttered foil

Ingredients:

1   3-ounce (85-gram) package cream cheese
2   cups (480 ml) confectioners' sugar, sifted
2   squares (2 ounces or 57 grams) unsweetened chocolate, melted
¼   teaspoon (1.25 ml) vanilla
Dash of salt
½   cup (120 ml) chopped pecans or walnuts

Preparation:

1. Have cream cheese at room temperature. Place in mixing bowl and cream with wooden spoon until smooth.

2. Slowly blend in the sugar.

3. Add melted chocolate and blend well.

4. Stir in vanilla, salt, and nuts. Continue stirring until mixture is blended.

5. Press into pan lined with lightly buttered foil.

6. Chill in refrigerator until firm.

7. Turn out onto smooth surface.

8. Remove foil and cut into 1-inch squares.

Yield: 1½ pounds (682 grams).

Variations:

Maple "Philly": Increase sugar to 2¾ cups (660 ml). Omit chocolate and vanilla. Substitute ¼ teaspoon (1.25 ml) maple flavoring or to taste.

Almond "Philly": Increase sugar to 2¾ cups (660 ml). Omit chocolate and vanilla. Substitute ¼ teaspoon (1.25 ml) almond extract. Omit pecans or walnuts. Substitute ½ cup (120 ml) chopped almonds, lightly roasted.

Coconut "Philly": Increase sugar to 3½ cups (840 ml). Omit chocolate and vanilla. Substitute ½ cup (120 ml) shredded coconut for the nuts.

Peanut Butter "Philly": Increase sugar to 2¾ cups (660 ml). Omit chocolate. Substitute 2 tablespoons (30 ml) creamy peanut butter. Omit pecans or walnuts. Substitute ¼ cup (60 ml) salted chopped peanuts.

French Chocolate Truffles

(Recommended as Centers for Chocolate or Summer Coating)

Chocolate truffles are considered a classic French sweetmeat. They are also a specialty in northern Italy where they are served in little fluted cups as one sips pungent expresso coffee.
    For a really wickedly delicious candy, dip the truffles in melted chocolate and then roll in cocoa, shredded coconut, or ground nuts.

Utensils:

1   1-quart double boiler
1   mixing bowl
1   set measuring spoons
1   set measuring cups
1   wooden spoon
1   large baking sheet lined with waxed paper

Ingredients:

3   (1-ounce or 28-gram) squares unsweetened chocolate
⅓   cup (80 ml) butter or margarine, softened
1¼ cups (300 ml) confectioners' sugar, sifted
3   large egg yolks
1   teaspoon (5 ml) vanilla
Melted chocolate, cocoa, coconut, or ground nuts

Preparation:

1. Melt the chocolate in the top of double boiler over hot water.

2. Combine butter and confectioners' sugar in mixing bowl; beat until smooth.

3. Beat in egg yolks one at a time.

4. Stir in chocolate and vanilla.

5. Chill until mixture is stiff; shape into ½-inch balls for dipping in melted chocolate or 1-inch balls for coating with cocoa, coconut, or ground nuts.

6. Place coated centers on baking sheet to firm.

Store in airtight container in cool, dry place.

Yield: Twenty-four 1-inch balls or forty-eight ½-inch balls.

Hazelnut Truffles

(Recommended as Centers for Chocolate or Summer Coating)

This recipe has won prizes in Indiana. Hazelnuts are the same as filberts.

Utensils:

1   1-quart double boiler
1   set measuring spoons
1   set measuring cups
1   wooden spoon
1   medium-size mixing bowl
1   large baking sheet lined with waxed paper

Ingredients:

2   cups (480 ml) chocolate bits
1   cup (240 ml) hazelnuts (filberts), lightly roasted and chopped
¾   cup (180 ml) sweetened condensed milk
Dash of salt
1   teaspoon (5 ml) vanilla
1½ cups (360 ml) chocolate sprinkles

Preparation:

1. Melt the chocolate bits in the top of double boiler over simmering water.

2. Remove from heat and stir in the hazelnuts, condensed milk, salt, and vanilla. Blend with wooden spoon until slightly thickened.

3. Cool for 5 minutes. The mixture should be cool enough to handle and hold its shape. It may be necessary to chill it in the refrigerator until firm.

4. With lightly buttered fingertips shape into ½-inch balls, then roll in chocolate sprinkles and place on baking sheet to dry for several hours.

Stored in airtight container they will keep for several months in freezer.

Yield: Sixty ½-inch balls.

Easy Chocolate Peanut Clusters

(Not Recommended as Centers for Coating)

This easy-to-do candy is very delicious! One of my friends in the Midwest sends all the way to New York for a regular supply.

Utensils:

1 1-quart double boiler
1 set measuring cups
1 wooden spoon
1 large baking sheet lined with waxed paper

Ingredients:

2 bars (4 ounces or 114 grams each) sweet cooking chocolate, or ½ pound (227 grams) chocolate bits
⅔ cup (160 ml) sweetened condensed milk
1 cup (240 ml) lightly roasted unsalted peanuts, or 1 cup (240 ml) raisins

Preparation:

1. Melt the chocolate in the top of double boiler over simmering water. Stir until smooth.

2. Remove from heat and blend in condensed milk and peanuts.

3. Drop by teaspoonfuls onto baking sheet.

4. Cool at room temperature until firm—2 to 3 hours.

Store in airtight container.

Yield: About 24 clusters.

Chapter 2
QUICK AND EASY FONDANT

In my workshops I begin by showing my students how to prepare uncomplicated fondants. Thus a novice can produce a variety of exciting and colorful candies with her very first attempt at the art of candy-making.

Quick Buttercrème Fondant

(Recommended as Centers for Chocolate, Summer, or Caramel Coating)

This is a delicious never-fail recipe for fondant that I picked up from the test kitchen of a company that produces high-quality flavorings and oils. Naturally enough, it calls for flavoring oil. (See Sources of Supply, p. 217.)

You can mold the fondant into the most intricate shapes before it cools. Follow instructions for molding marzipan, pp. 69-70.

Utensils:

1   large heavy saucepan
1   set measuring spoons
1   set measuring cups
1   wooden spoon
1   large baking sheet with sides

Ingredients:

⅓   cup (80 ml) butter or margarine
½   cup (120 ml) light corn syrup
4¼ cups (1020 ml) (1 pound) (454 grams) confectioners' sugar, sifted
1   teaspoon (5 ml) vanilla or use ¼ teaspoon (1.25 ml) flavoring oil
Food coloring (optional) (See Coloring and Flavoring Charts, pp. 30-31.)

Preparation:

1. Combine the butter, corn syrup, and one-half the sugar in saucepan.

2. Cook over low heat, stirring constantly with wooden spoon until mixture comes to a full boil (about 5 minutes).

3. Add the remaining sugar and continue stirring over low heat until well blended.

4. Remove from heat and stir until mixture holds its shape and becomes rather thick. Add vanilla and optional food coloring.

5. Turn onto dampened baking sheet and cool to lukewarm.

6. Knead with the hands until creamy but still warm to the touch.

7. Shape with lightly buttered hands into balls, mint-size patties, etc.

8. Place on waxed paper to cool.

These can be eaten at once, unlike cooked fondant which needs a ripening period. They may also be dipped in coating as soon as they have cooled to room temperature. They will keep, stored in airtight containers in the refrigerator or freezer, for about 1 month.

Yield: Approximately one hundred ½-inch centers to be dipped in coating.

Variations:

Quick Fondant Balls: Use ⅓ of cooked recipe. Knead in additional flavoring to taste. Form into ½-inch balls and roll in finely ground nuts or finely grated semisweet chocolate. Store in airtight plastic bags.

Rum-Walnut Creams: Use ⅓ of cooked recipe. Knead in 1 teaspoon (5 ml) high-quality cocoa and 1 teaspoon (5 ml) rum flavoring. Form into ½-inch balls. Elongate them slightly to form ovals and then top with a walnut quarter.

Cherry Fondant Hearts: Use ⅓ of cooked recipe. Knead in 1 teaspoon (5 ml) cherry flavoring, 1 teaspoon (5 ml) lemon juice, and a few drops of red coloring. Roll out on waxed paper and cut into heart shapes with small cookie cutter or mold the hearts by hand.

Decorate the center of each heart with candied cherry half.

Coffee Creams: Use ⅓ of cooked recipe. Knead in 5 teaspoons (25 ml) instant powdered coffee. Form into ½-inch balls.

Quick and Easy Easter-Egg Centers: Double fondant recipe. Add 1 cup (240 ml) flaked or shredded coconut and 4 cups (960 ml) chopped pecans. Form into ovals not more than 2 inches in length. Larger ones would be difficult to dip in coating.

Yield: 24 medium-size eggs.

Dolley Madisons

(Recommended as Centers for Chocolate or Summer Coating)

Dolley Madisons, *sometimes known as* Martha Washingtons, *are an old Southern tradition. They have a tasty uncooked fondant base coated with milk chocolate and topped with a large pecan half.*

An old recipe, with complicated, archaic directions, ends by saying, "This is a good recipe for the inexperienced candy-maker." The following version is in modern culinary language, but still has the original historic ingredients, and is a good recipe for beginners.

Save a special antique compote for a cherished friend and give it to her on May 20, filled with Dolley Madisons, to celebrate the birthday of the elegant hostess.

Utensils:

2 large mixing bowls
Electric mixer (optional)
1 set measuring spoons
1 set measuring cups
1 wooden spoon
1 large baking sheet

Ingredients:

5 cups (1200 ml) confectioners' sugar, sifted
½ cup (120 ml) (1 stick) salted butter, softened
1 egg white, stiffly beaten
1½ teaspoons (7.5 ml) pure vanilla extract
46 perfect pecan halves

Preparation:

1. Combine 2½ cups (600 ml) confectioners' sugar with the softened butter in one bowl.

2. Combine the remaining sugar with the stiffly beaten egg white in the other bowl.

3. Cream the mixtures in both bowls as if making cake.

4. When both mixtures are thoroughly creamed, combine them in one bowl and add the vanilla.

5. Knead the mixture into a ball.

6. Turn out onto damp surface of baking sheet and continue to knead until light and creamy.

7. Wrap fondant ball in waxed paper and store in airtight container to ripen for at least 24 hours.

These centers are traditionally formed into ½-inch balls. Hand-dip in milk chocolate and top with a pecan half.

Yield: Approximately 46 centers.

Kentucky Colonels

(Recommended as Centers for Chocolate Coating)

"Kentucky Colonel" is an honorary title bestowed upon famous people from that state and it is also the name of a special chocolate-coated bourbon-flavored fondant. Recipes abound, but this one has been tested for the at-home candymaker. A delicious and sophisticated candy to serve any time. But beware! Federal laws prohibit selling these candies outside the state of Kentucky.

Utensils:

1   large mixing bowl
Electric mixer
1   set measuring cups
1   wooden spoon
1   large baking sheet

Ingredients:

¼   cup (60 ml) (½ stick) butter, softened
4   cups (960 ml) (one pound or 454 grams) confectioners' sugar, sifted
¼   cup (60 ml) good-quality bourbon
2   cups (480 ml) pecans, chopped

Preparation:

1. Place butter in mixing bowl.

2. Set mixer for slow speed, and gradually add sugar, ¼ cup (60 ml) at a time, alternately with 1 teaspoon (5 ml) of bourbon. Continue this procedure until all sugar and bourbon are used.

3. Remove beaters and stir in pecans with a wooden spoon.

4. Form into ½-inch balls.

5. Place on lightly greased baking sheet and chill in refrigerator overnight, or for at least 4 hours.

These centers are usually dipped in the dark chocolate coating because of the richness of the bourbon-flavored centers.

Old-Fashioned Potato Fondant

(Recommended as Centers for Chocolate, Summer, or Caramel Coating)

Uncooked potato fondant is an old pioneer recipe, so old no one knows its source. I received this from an elderly lady in Kentucky, who wrote, "It was given to me by my grandmother, who always served it in little frilly cups or used it as a base for mint patties at Christmas time."

Utensils:

1   large mixing bowl
1   set measuring spoons
1   set measuring cups
1   wooden spoon
Electric mixer (optional)
1   large baking sheet

Ingredients:

½   cup (120 ml) mashed potatoes, unseasoned—not instant
3   cups (720 ml) confectioners' sugar, sifted
1   cup (240 ml) moist coconut, flaked or shredded
1   teaspoon (5 ml) vanilla

Preparation:

1. Combine mashed potatoes, sugar, coconut, and vanilla in mixing bowl.

2. Cream with wooden spoon or electric mixer as for making cake.

3. Chill mixture in refrigerator several hours.

4. Remove and turn onto damp surface of baking sheet.

5. Knead with hands until the mixture is creamy.

6. Shape into 1-inch balls.

7. Serve in crinkle cups available from confectioners' supply house (see Sources of Supply, p. 217). Or make your own (see p. 215).

Store in airtight container for approximately 2 weeks.

Yield: Approximately 1½ pounds (682 grams) or sixty 1-inch balls.

Variations:

Tennessee Christmas Mints: Omit vanilla and substitute a few drops of oil of peppermint. Tint fondant pink with food coloring. Flatten balls to approximately ¼-inch thickness.

Candied-Fruit Balls: Omit vanilla and substitute rum, lemon, or maple flavoring. Add ½ cup (120 ml) finely chopped candied fruit such as cherries, pineapple, apricots, or dates. Dried orange or lemon peel can also be used. Allow confections to dry at room temperature for at least 24 hours. These keep well at room temperature for 2 weeks if covered with plastic wrap.

Filbert Squares: Add ¾ cup (180 ml) chopped unsalted filberts, lightly toasted, to recipe while kneading mixture. Roll out onto smooth surface into a square approximately 1 inch thick. Cut into individual ¾-inch squares.

Coffee Mocha Logs: Add 2 teaspoons (10 ml) instant powdered coffee to recipe while kneading mixture. Shape into finger rolls ½ x 2 inches. Roll in chocolate sprinkles.

Peanut-Butter Balls

(Recommended as Centers for Chocolate Coating)

The recipe given here is a contribution from the home economics department of a high school in Martinsville, Virginia. A longtime favorite with students, faculty, and PTA, the chocolate-coated peanut-butter balls appear in quantity at virtually all the school's functions. I recommend them as candies to be made for profit, bazaars, or charity benefits.

Utensils:

1   large mixing bowl
1   set measuring cups
1   wooden spoon
1   large baking sheet lined with waxed paper

Ingredients:

4   tablespoons (60 ml) butter, softened
1½ cups (360 ml) confectioners' sugar, sifted
¾   cup (180 ml) creamy-style peanut butter

Preparation:

1. Combine butter, sugar, and peanut butter in mixing bowl and stir with wooden spoon until blended. Do not use electric mixer because over-mixing will cause the centers to be too soft for dipping.

2. With the fingertips shape mixture into ½-inch balls and place on baking sheet lined with waxed paper.

3. Refrigerate for a few hours until firm.

4. Remove and let stand at room temperature for 30 minutes before dipping.

Yield: About fifty-four ½-inch balls.

Flavored-Gelatin Easter-Egg Centers

(Recommended as Centers for Chocolate or Summer Coating)

The following recipe came to me from the wife of an Army man stationed in the Philippines where fresh coconut abounds. It proved to be a very good and very satisfactory way to make a variety of egg centers, because one is free to choose any color, depending on the flavor of gelatin used, and the result is always deliciously tart and not too rich. Start your Easter-egg collection with this base.

Utensils:

1	large mixing bowl
1	set measuring spoons
1	set measuring cups
1	wooden spoon
1	large baking sheet lined with waxed paper

Ingredients:

2	cups (480 ml) flaked or shredded coconut Toast lightly if using freshly grated
1	package (3 ounces) (85 grams) fruit gelatin, any flavor
1	cup (240 ml) chopped pecans, walnuts, or roasted blanched almonds
1½	teaspoons (7.5 ml) sugar
²/₃	cup (160 ml) sweetened condensed milk
1	teaspoon (5 ml) almond extract

Preparation:

1. Combine all the ingredients in mixing bowl.

2. Stir with wooden spoon to blend.

3. Turn onto dampened baking sheet and knead with the hands until smooth and creamy.

4. Shape into 1 large, 2 medium, or 12 small eggs.

5. Chill in refrigerator until firm and dry on outside.

6. Remove from refrigerator and let come to room temperature before dipping.

Note: This recipe may be doubled for making centers in quantity.

Yield: Ten 2-inch eggs.

Variation:

Strawberries: Use strawberry-flavored gelatin. Omit nuts. With the fingertips mold into strawberry shapes. Roll in red sugar sprinkles. Cut off the green cellophane fringed end of a fancy toothpick and use for stem. These are very beautiful and easy to do for bazaars and benefit sales.

Yield: About 48 strawberries.

Chapter 3
QUICK AND EASY
CANDY-TYPE CONFECTIONS
(Made with Crushed Wafers)

Use these sweets to embellish midafternoon tea, a holiday punch bowl, or for gift giving. Because they have a base of crushed wafers, they keep very well, especially if you store them between layers of waxed paper in an airtight container. Pack in imaginative containers for gift giving. (See special section for gift-wrapping candies, pp. 202-216.)

Bourbon Balls

(Recommended as Centers for Chocolate or Summer Coating)

Bourbon balls are from Kentucky where they always appear at Christmas when many families have open house and on Derby Day. I serve them to my European friends, who consider bourbon a very sophisticated flavoring.

Utensils:

1   large mixing bowl
1   set measuring spoons
1   set measuring cups
1   wooden spoon
1   large baking sheet lined with waxed paper

Ingredients:

1   cup (240 ml) (about 32) vanilla or chocolate wafers, crushed
1   cup (240 ml) confectioners' sugar, sifted
1   cup (240 ml) pecans or hickory nuts, chopped
2   tablespoons (30 ml) cocoa
1½ tablespoons (22.5 ml) light corn syrup
¼   cup (60 ml) good bourbon whiskey or rum
Confectioners' sugar for coating

Preparation:

1. Combine crushed wafers, sugar, nuts, and cocoa in mixing bowl.

2. Stir with wooden spoon until blended.

3. Add corn syrup and bourbon and continue to blend until thoroughly mixed.

4. With fingertips shape into 1-inch balls. Roll in sugar and place on baking sheet to dry for several hours.

5. Keep in airtight container to ripen for 2 to 3 days.

Like fruit cake, these improve with age and may be frozen up to 6 months.

Yield: Thirty-six 1-inch balls.

Orange Balls

(Recommended as Centers for Chocolate or Summer Coating)

This recipe is also Southern, from an elegant Atlanta hostess who serves these with her special New Year's punch at her annual open house. They also provide a piquant contrast with a cup of good tea. A can of choice tea and attractively wrapped Orange Balls *make a gift to delight any connoisseur of food.*

Utensils:

1   1-quart double boiler
1   set measuring spoons
1   set measuring cups
1   large mixing bowl
1   wooden spoon
1   large baking sheet lined with waxed paper

Ingredients:

1   cup (240 ml) butterscotch bits
½   cup (120 ml) granulated sugar
3   tablespoons (45 ml) light corn syrup
½   cup (120 ml) frozen orange juice concentrate, undiluted
2⅔ cups (640 ml) vanilla wafers, crushed
1   cup (240 ml) pecans or walnuts, finely chopped
Granulated sugar for coating

Preparation:

1. Melt butterscotch bits in top of double boiler over simmering water, stirring with wooden spoon until smooth.

2. Add sugar, corn syrup, and orange juice. Continue stirring until blended.

3. In mixing bowl combine crushed wafers, pecans, and butterscotch mixture. Mix well with wooden spoon.

4. With fingertips shape into 1-inch balls. Roll in sugar and place on baking sheet to dry for several hours.

5. Keep in airtight container to ripen for 2 to 3 days.

These may be frozen up to 6 months.

Yield: Sixty 1-inch balls.

Nut Chocolate Drops (Nupgeback)

(Not Recommended as Centers for Coating)

Making confections with crushed wafers probably began years ago in Germany where they became a favorite sweet made for New Year's Eve.

In the Rhineland they use crushed braune pfeffernusse as a base. However, I use crushed gingersnap wafers as a more available and just-as-good substitute.

Utensils:

1   1-quart double boiler
1   set measuring spoons
1   wooden spoon
1   spatula
1   baking sheet lined with waxed paper

Ingredients:

8   ounces (227 grams) *sweet* German chocolate
4   tablespoons (60 ml) evaporated milk, undiluted
4   tablespoons (60 ml) crushed gingersnap wafers
4   tablespoons (60 ml) confectioners' sugar, sifted
4   tablespoons (60 ml) lightly roasted blanched almonds, chopped
½   teaspoon (2.5 ml) vanilla or almond extract

Preparation:

1. Melt chocolate in the top of double boiler over simmering water.

2. Stir in the milk, gingersnaps, sugar, nuts, and vanilla. Blend well with wooden spoon.

3. Drop from teaspoon onto waxed paper and flatten slightly with buttered spatula.

4. Cool for several hours and store in airtight container to ripen for 2 to 3 days.

5. Serve in small fluted cups.

Yield: Approximately 20 rounds.

Peanut Rum Balls

(Not Recommended as Centers for Coating)

Orange- and peanut-flavored confections make a tasty combination to serve on your prettiest silver candy dish at teatime.

Utensils:

1   large mixing bowl
1   set measuring spoons
1   set measuring cups
1   wooden spoon
1   large baking sheet lined with waxed paper

Ingredients:

2½ cups (600 ml) (about 5½ dozen, small) vanilla wafers, crushed
1   cup (240 ml) confectioners' sugar, sifted
½   cup (120 ml) roasted unsalted peanuts, chopped
2   tablespoons (30 ml) cocoa, preferably Dutch
3   tablespoons (45 ml) light corn syrup
¼   cup (60 ml) good dark rum
Confectioners' sugar for coating

Preparation:

1. Combine crushed wafers and 1 cup (240 ml) sugar in mixing bowl.

2. Add peanuts and cocoa and stir well with wooden spoon.

3. Add corn syrup and rum and continue stirring until well mixed.

4. With fingertips shape into 1-inch balls. Roll in sugar and place on baking sheet to dry for several hours.

5. Keep in airtight container to ripen for 2 to 3 days.

These may be frozen up to 6 months.

Yield: Thirty-six 1-inch balls.

Holiday Fruit Balls

(Not Recommended as Centers for Coating)

Utensils:

1   large mixing bowl
1   2-quart saucepan
1   set measuring spoons
1   set measuring cups
1   wooden spoon

Ingredients:

1   cup (240 ml) chopped pecans
¾   cup (180 ml) candied cherries, quartered
1   cup (240 ml) (½ pound or 227 grams) pitted dates, chopped
3½ cups (840 ml) crushed graham crackers
1   cup (240 ml) marshmallow crème
1   tablespoon (15 ml) grated orange rind
¼   cup (60 ml) fresh orange juice
¼   teaspoon (1.25 ml) each ground cinnamon, nutmeg, cloves, allspice, and ginger
1   cup (240 ml) pecans or 1 cup (240 ml) flaked coconut for coating

Preparation:

1. Combine 1 cup (240 ml) nuts, cherries, the dates, and crushed graham crackers in mixing bowl; set aside.

2. Combine the marshmallow crème, orange rind, juice, and spices in saucepan.

3. Stir with wooden spoon over low heat until crème is melted and mixture is blended.

4. Pour over nut-fruit mixture and blend well; chill for 2 to 3 hours or until firm.

5. With fingertips shape into 1-inch balls. Roll in the remaining nuts or coconut. Wrap individually in plastic wrap.

Store in airtight container. Can be frozen up to 6 months.

Yield: Eighty-four balls.

Chapter 4
QUICK AND EASY CEREAL CONFECTIONS

Make some cereal confections in a jiffy! They are not only quick to prepare, but also delicious and festive. I call them "gifts of the moment" because they lend themselves to kooky and imaginative gift-wrapping ideas. Especially great for young parties and a limited budget. Skrunches are fun to make and even more fun to give away.

Cornflake Penuche

(Not Recommended as Centers for Coating)

This recipe produced interesting reactions in my kitchen. Fresh, it was chewy to the point of being tough and my teen-age testers discarded it as a "turkey." We covered the pan with waxed paper and two days later the contents had turned crisp and crunchy, at which point the testers devoured the whole batch.

Utensils:

1   4-quart saucepan
1   set measuring cups
1   wooden spoon
1   square pan, 8 x 8 x 2 inches, lined with
    buttered foil

Ingredients:

3   tablespoons (45 ml) butter or margarine
1¼ cups (300 ml) light brown sugar, firmly
    packed
⅓ cup (80 ml) evaporated milk, undiluted
5   cups (1200 ml) cornflakes

Preparation:

1. Melt the butter in saucepan over low heat.

2. Add sugar and stir with wooden spoon, mixing well until sugar is dissolved.

3. Stir and very slowly add the milk.

4. Keep the heat low and add the cornflakes. Stir until well mixed.

5. Remove from heat and press into prepared pan.

6. Cover loosely with waxed paper. Let stand for 48 hours in cool, dry place but do not refrigerate.

7. Turn candy out onto smooth surface. Remove foil and break into eating-size pieces.

Store in airtight container for no longer than 3 to 4 days.

Yield: Approximately 1 pound (454 grams).

Chocolate Caramel Skrunch

(Not Recommended as Centers for Coating)

Utensils:

1   1-quart milk carton with top removed
1   large mixing bowl
1   1-quart heavy iron saucepan
1   set measuring spoons
1   set measuring cups
1   wooden spoon
1   narrow spatula

Ingredients:

2   cups (480 ml) cornflakes
1   cup (240 ml) crisp rice cereal
½   cup (120 ml) chocolate bits
1   cup (240 ml) broken nuts, any kind but peanuts
¾   cup (180 ml) dark corn syrup
¼   cup (60 ml) granulated sugar
2   tablespoons (30 ml) butter or margarine
½   teaspoon (2.5 ml) vanilla

Preparation:

1. Combine cereals, chocolate bits, and nuts in mixing bowl; set aside.

2. Combine corn syrup, sugar, and butter in saucepan.

3. Bring to full boil over medium heat, stirring constantly with wooden spoon, and boil for 3 minutes.

4. Remove from heat. Cool for 10 minutes.

5. Add vanilla. Beat mixture with wooden spoon until syrup turns light brown and thickens.

6. Pour immediately over cereal mixture. Toss to coat evenly.

7. With lightly buttered fingers press firmly into milk carton.

8. Chill in refrigerator for 1 to 2 hours or until firm.

9. Loosen with spatula and slip out of carton.

10. Slice into eating-size squares about 1-inch thick. Wrap in plastic wrap.

Store in airtight container for not more than 1 week.

Yield: Approximately 1 pound (454 grams).

Variations:

Butterscotch Skrunch: Omit chocolate bits. Substitute butterscotch bits.

Mocha Skrunch: Add 1 tablespoon (15 ml) instant coffee powder to corn syrup, sugar, and butter before boiling.

Peanut and Raisin Skrunch: Omit chocolate bits. Substitute ½ cup (120 ml) raisins. Omit nuts. Substitute 1 cup (240 ml) chopped peanuts. Add 1 teaspoon (5 ml) ground cinnamon to the corn syrup, sugar, and butter before boiling.

Peanut Butter Skrunch: Increase rice cereal to 2 cups (480 ml). Omit nuts. Add ½ cup (120 ml) chunky-style peanut butter to the corn syrup, sugar, and butter before boiling. Omit vanilla. Substitute almond extract.

To Mold or Make Free Forms: Follow instructions for making candied popcorn decorations (p. 142).

Chapter 5
QUICK AND EASY DRIED-FRUIT CONFECTIONS

This class of goodies is without limit if you are inventive.

Dried-fruit confections are becoming increasingly popular in place of sugar candy, especially among parents interested in healthy nutrition for their children.

When you select the dried fruits, consider the way you will use them. To combine with a candy-box assortment, choose small-size fruit. Big fancy prunes, dates, figs, and apricots are too large to look dainty in a box of candy.

Various mixtures are good for stuffing fruits, but nuts, or combinations of fruit, nuts, and fondant, blend best with the flavors of dried fruits.

When stuffing dried fruits, fill them only moderately full. Over-stuffed fruits become too large; they are unappetizing and difficult to eat.

Candied cherries may be stuffed with nuts, fondant, almond paste, or any fruit mixture. Use a sharp knife to make two slits crossing each other at right angles, and each cutting halfway through the cherry, so four sections can be brought up around the stuffing to form petals. These can be used most effectively to fill in the chinks of a candy-box assortment and at the same time add a dash of color and style. A whole blanched almond may be inserted in each cherry, making an acorn-shaped confection. The cherry may be rolled in tiny colored-sugar sprinkles, which will adhere to the cherry but not to the nut.

Fondant mixed with nuts, or nuts and crystallized apricots, may be used as stuffing for all dried fruit. Any butter-flavored fondant is especially good.

Almond paste, mixed with any fondant in the proportion of two parts paste to one of fondant, may be used for stuffing all dried fruit.

Persian Sweets

(Recommended as Centers for Chocolate or Fondant Coating)

This is an old-fashioned recipe, sometimes called Persian balls or centers. You can dip them in Chocolate or Fondant Coating, or use them to stuff dried fruits.

Utensils:

Food grinder or food processor
1   pastry board
1   set measuring spoons
1   set measuring cups
1   large baking sheet lined with waxed paper

Ingredients:

¾   cup (180 ml) dried figs, stems removed before measuring
¾   cup (180 ml) dried dates, pitted before measuring
¾   cup (180 ml) walnuts, chopped
Confectioners' sugar for coating pastry board
2   tablespoons (30 ml) orange rind, grated
1 to 2 tablespoons (15-30 ml) fresh lemon juice
1   cup (240 ml) walnut halves for garnish

Preparation:

1. Steam figs and dates, if they're too dry.

2. Grind the figs, dates, and walnuts together twice, using finest blade of food grinder.

3. Spread the mixture on pastry board coated with confectioners' sugar.

4. Sprinkle the mixture with the grated orange rind and lemon juice; knead thoroughly until it forms a smooth paste.

5. Form into a long sausage-shape roll 1 inch thick and, with a sharp knife dipped in sugar, cut the roll into ½-inch slices.

6. Coat each slice with additional sugar, top with a walnut half, and place on waxed paper to dry for 2 to 3 hours or until firm.

To make balls or centers, cut the slices in half before coating with sugar and with the fingertips roll into small balls. When firm, dip in coating.

Store in airtight container in cool, dry place. May be frozen up to 6 months.

Yield: Fifteen slices or thirty 1-inch balls.

Apricot-Coconut Balls

(Recommended as Centers for Chocolate or Summer Coating)

The following is a tart-sweet classic confection recipe for apricot lovers. Dip each piece in Chocolate or Summer Coating or roll in confectioners' sugar.

Utensils:

1   large mixing bowl
1   set measuring spoons
1   set measuring cups
1   wooden spoon
1   large baking sheet lined with waxed paper

Ingredients:

2   tablespoons (30 ml) butter or margarine
½   cup (120 ml) light corn syrup
1   tablespoon (15 ml) water
½   teaspoon (2.5 ml) vanilla
¼   teaspoon (1.25 ml) almond extract
⅔   cup (160 ml) instant nonfat dry milk solids
2   cups (480 ml) dried apricots, finely chopped
2   cups (480 ml) flaked coconut
Confectioners' sugar for coating

Preparation:

1. Combine butter and corn syrup in mixing bowl; stir in water, flavorings, dry milk solids, apricots, and coconut.

2. Knead mixture until thoroughly blended.

3. Shape into ½-inch balls for dipping in Chocolate or Summer Coating or form into 1-inch balls for coating in sugar.

Yield: Thirty 1-inch balls or sixty ½-inch balls.

Stuffing Dates

From Nan Wiley's "Let's Ask the Cook" newspaper column: "They're good, they're easy to prepare and they make a nice contrast for any candy plate."

Preparation:

1. Soak dates in sweet wine or orange juice just to cover, but don't drown them. They pick up nice additional flavor and stay moist. Or, if they seem on the dry side, you may steam them first for a few minutes before soaking.

2. Carefully remove date pits. (Pitted dates may be used, but the others seem to hold their shape better.)

3. Stuff with nut halves, quartered marshmallows, candied ginger, candied pineapple, salted almonds, or peanut butter moistened with orange juice. Roll in confectioners' or granulated sugar. My favorite way is to stuff them with fondant and top with a pecan half.

Turkish Sweetmeats

(Not Recommended as Centers for Coating)

These old-fashioned sweets take on a modern new look with a Quick Buttercrème Fondant. *Make them by the gross for family treats and for gift giving.*

Utensils:

2 small mixing bowls
1 set measuring spoons
1 set measuring cups
2 wooden spoons
1 pastry tube with star tip
1 large baking sheet lined with waxed
   paper

Ingredients:

Recipe Quick Buttercreme Fondant
(p. 42)
1 teaspoon (5 ml) grated lemon rind
1 teaspoon (5 ml) grated lime rind
Yellow and green food coloring
1 cup (240 ml) (one 8-oz. package or 227
   grams) pitted dates
1 cup (240 ml) (one 8-oz. package or 227
   grams) dried apricots

Preparation:

1. Reheat fondant and divide between 2 small bowls; add lemon rind to one bowl and lime rind to the second bowl.

2. Tint the lemon fondant with a few drops yellow food coloring and the lime fondant with a few drops green food coloring.

3. Fit the star tip into pastry bag; fill with lemon fondant.

4. Pipe fondant into each date. Arrange in rows on prepared baking sheet.

5. Rinse and dry pastry bag and tip.

6. Refit bag with tip and fill with lime fondant.

7. Pipe fondant onto half the apricots, top with remaining apricots.

8. Arrange with dates on baking sheet.

9. Store in refrigerator until serving time.

Yield: 2 pounds (909 grams).

Note: Hand-carry these as hostess gifts. Do not ship by mail.

Chapter 6
MARSHMALLOWS AND JELLY CANDIES

Marshmallows are an Egyptian confection originally made from thorn-tree gum or sap, a binding ingredient known today as gum arabic and still used by commercial marshmallow manufacturers. The gum is not an ingredient you will need. You can make a more tender fluffy marshmallow than the commercial variety with un-flavored gelatin, sugar, corn syrup, and flavoring.

Marshmallows are uncooked candies and you must use an electric mixer; it is almost impossible to beat a marshmallow mass by hand. In fact, only the electric hand mixer makes it possible to make the candy successfully at home. When I was young, I had an aunt who continually tried to make marshmallows with a rotary hand beater. Never was the result anything but tacky and gluey.

Uncooked marshmallows are true candy-pan magic. Four simple ingredients unfold before your eyes into fluffy white confections. Here is an excellent first candy-making lesson for youngsters or the not so young who are looking for an easy way to create delicious candy.

Jelly candies can be made at home! Strange as it seems, they are part of the marshmallow family.

Depending upon freshness of color and flavoring, jellies are favorites among young and old during both the hot summer months and the winter holiday season. The finished sweet should be firm on the outside, but soft when you bite into it.

Uncooked Marshmallows

(Recommended as Centers for Chocolate or Summer Coating)

Utensils:

Electric mixer
1　large mixing bowl
1　small saucepan for dissolving gelatin
1　set measuring spoons
1　set measuring cups
1　wooden spoon
1　large baking sheet with sides
1　square pan 8 x 8 x 2 inches
Scissors

Ingredients:

4　teaspoons (20 ml) unflavored gelatin
⅓　cup (80 ml) cold water
½　cup (120 ml) granulated sugar
⅔　cup (160 ml) light corn syrup
½　teaspoon (2.5 ml) vanilla
½　cup (120 ml) confectioners' sugar
　　combined with ½ cup (120 ml)
　　cornstarch

Preparation:

1. Put the gelatin into saucepan. Add the cold water and stir well with wooden spoon to dissolve.

2. Let stand for 5 minutes, until mixture becomes firm.

3. Liquefy the mixture over hot water.

4. Add the granulated sugar to the warm gelatin and stir well.

5. Pour mixture into mixing bowl and add corn syrup and vanilla.

6. Beat the mixture on HI speed for 15

minutes, no cheating. The marshmallow mixture will be very thick and fluffy.

7. Lightly butter the square pan and sprinkle liberally with combined sugar and cornstarch.

8. Pour marshmallow mixture into pan. Smooth top surface and place in the refrigerator overnight or for several hours to firm.

9. Remove from the refrigerator and sprinkle top surface with more of the combined sugar and cornstarch.

10. Loosen sides and bottom of the marshmallow square with a spatula, or use your hands to remove it from pan in one piece.

11. Turn out onto baking sheet coated with more of the confectioners' sugar-cornstarch mixture. The marshmallow will be rather sticky until thoroughly coated.

12. Dip scissors in cold water and cut marshmallow into 1-inch squares.

13. Roll each piece in sugar-cornstarch coating and place on rack to dry for several hours.

These will stay moist in airtight container for approximately 3 weeks.

Yield: Sixty-four 1-inch squares.

Variations:

Tinted Marshmallows: Marshmallows may be tinted any desired color. Any flavoring may be substituted for the vanilla. See Coloring and Flavoring Charts (pp. 30-31).

Toasted Coconut Marshmallows: Omit confectioners' sugar-cornstarch mixture. Instead lightly butter the square pan and coat bottom with 1 cup (240 ml) lightly toasted coconut. Pour in marshmallow mixture and sprinkle 1 more cup (240 ml) of lightly toasted coconut on top surface. When firm, cut into 1-inch squares and coat sides with more toasted coconut.

Crème de Menthe Marshmallows: Omit vanilla and substitute peppermint extract or a few drops of oil of peppermint. Tint pastel green.

Chocolate-Coconut Marshmallows: Omit vanilla and add 2 tablespoons (30 ml) cocoa and 1 teaspoon (5 ml) chocolate-flavored extract. Coat with lightly toasted coconut as for *Toasted Coconut Marshmallows* (above).

Fruit-Flavored Marshmallows: Dissolve gelatin in equal quantity of fresh fruit juice, omitting water. Use any flavor of juice except fresh pineapple. Tint appropriate color with a few drops of food coloring. See Coloring and Flavoring Charts (pp. 30-31).

Fruit-and-Nut Marshmallows: Add 1 cup chopped nuts, dates, figs, raisins, or candied cherries with the vanilla. A combination of fruits and nuts is very tasty.

Sugar-Coated Marshmallows: Omit confectioners' sugar-cornstarch mixture coating and substitute colored-sugar sprinkles.

Cutting and Shaping Marshmallows:

Marshmallow chicks, bunnies, eggs, et cetera, are best known as Easter candies. To make your own, prepare several batches of uncooked marshmallow and leave it in the refrigerator until time to form shapes.

Use cookie cutters if you do not feel adept at cutting free forms. Cutting and hand-shaping uncoated marshmallow is an unbelievably sticky chore unless you keep hands, scissors, or cutters wet at all times. Keep a bowl of ice water nearby for this purpose. Roll each form in coating as soon as it is shaped and place it on rack to dry.

The forms may be dipped in Chocolate or Summer Coating. They are also very colorful if rolled in colored-sugar sprinkles.

Molding Marshmallow Forms:

Special molds may be ordered from a confectioners' supply house. (See Sources of Supply, p. 217.) However, if you look around your kitchen you will probably find suitable containers, or buy some inexpensive foil molds from the supermarket. A 1-pound canned-ham tin makes a beautiful Easter egg. Just make sure the edges of the tin are not sharp.

Preparation:

1. Prepare the tins by first lightly coating them with butter, and then sprinkling liberally with a combination of confectioners' sugar and cornstarch.

2. Shake the excess from mold; pour in marshmallow and smooth the surface.

3. Cool in refrigerator until firm.

4. Unmold and coat with tinted coconut or sugar sprinkles.

The larger the mold, the easier it is to handle the form to be coated. A white marshmallow lamb may be coated with white shredded coconut to give him a nice fleecy Easter look. With a little practice you will be turning out professional-looking Easter candies for decorations and gift giving.

Variations:

Marshmallows with Chocolate or Summer Coating: Do not use bonbon or caramel coating because homemade marshmallows are too soft and tender to withstand the high temperature of the dipping mixture. Prepare marshmallow and cut into 1-inch squares, or smaller squares if they are to be used in a candy-box assortment. Coat with a combination of confectioners' sugar and cornstarch. Let dry on racks for at least 24 hours at room temperature. Shake excess coating from squares and dip in either light or dark Chocolate Coating or in Summer Coating. Each marshmallow square may be garnished with a nut half. A box of these makes a handsome and rather inexpensive gift.

Marshmallow Candy Bars: Prepare recipe for *Uncooked Marshmallows.* Cut marshmallow into bars 1 inch wide and 2½ inches in length. Coat with a combination of confectioners' sugar and cornstarch. Let dry on rack overnight. Shake off excess coating and dip in light or dark Chocolate or Summer Coating. The chocolate-coated bars may be garnished with nut halves, chopped nuts, coconut, et cetera. Those with the frosty Summer Coating may be decorated by using a pastry tube.

Yield: 24 candy bars.

Rocky Roads

(Not Recommended as Centers for Coating)

A famous Miami Beach candy boutique packs these by the box and calls them a Florida specialty, but they were also native to the Midwest when I grew up there. They are just a basic milk chocolate with nuts and marshmallows. Make your own marshmallows for that special touch.

Utensils:

1   square pan, 8 x 8 x 2 inches, lined with foil
1   1-quart double boiler
1   set measuring cups
1   wooden spoon

Ingredients:

1   pound (454 grams) rich milk chocolate, coarsely chopped

1   cup (240 ml) pecans or walnuts
12   marshmallows cut into 1-inch squares and then into ¼-inch squares

Preparation:

1. Melt the chocolate in top of double boiler over simmering water. Keep heat low. Stir mixture with wooden spoon until smooth.

2. Remove from heat and pour half the mixture onto the foil-lined pan.

3. Keep the remaining chocolate warm.

4. Arrange the nuts and marshmallows evenly over the chocolate layer.

5. Pour the remaining chocolate over the nuts and marshmallows. Cool until firm.

6. Turn out onto smooth surface and cut into eating-size pieces.

This confection will stay fresh for weeks if left in one piece and wrapped securely with foil. Cut off what you wish and rewrap. This makes an attractive gift for mailing if molded in foil-lined ice-cube tray and tied with a gay ribbon bow.

Note: 12 large-size commercial marshmallows may be quartered and used.

Yield: 1½ pounds (682 grams).

Basic Jelly Candies

(Recommended as Centers for Chocolate or Summer Coating)

The following basic recipe for jelly candies gives you a pretty bright-yellow addition to any candy-box assortment—light-textured candies with a tart and sweet flavor.

Utensils:

1   2-quart heavy saucepan
1   small mixing bowl
1   set measuring spoons
1   set measuring cups
1   small sieve
1   wooden spoon
1   spatula
1   strainer
1   loaf pan, 9 x 5 x 3 inches, well oiled
1   baking sheet with sides, lightly oiled

Ingredients:

3   tablespoons (45 ml) (3 envelopes) unflavored gelatin
½   cup (120 ml) cold water
½   cup (120 ml) hot water
2   cups (480 ml) granulated sugar
6   drops yellow food coloring
¼   cup (60 ml) orange juice
2   tablespoons (30 ml) lemon juice
2   tablespoons (30 ml) grated orange rind (1 large orange)
1   tablespoon (15 ml) grated lemon rind (1 large lemon)
Granulated or confectioners' sugar for coating

Preparation:

1. Combine the gelatin and cold water in mixing bowl. Let stand for at least 5 minutes.

2. Meanwhile combine the hot water and sugar in saucepan and place over low heat.

3. Stir until sugar grains are dissolved, but do not let mixture boil. You should not be able to feel sugar grains when you rub the wooden spoon against the side of the pan.

4. Remove from heat and add gelatin mixture and food coloring, stirring constantly until thoroughly mixed.

5. Return to moderate heat and boil mixture slowly for *20 minutes.* Set timer, if necessary.

6. Remove from heat and add citrus juices and rind. Stir for a few seconds to extract the oil from the lemon and orange rinds.

7. Strain mixture into well-oiled loaf pan. Chill in refrigerator until firm.

8. Turn out onto lightly oiled baking sheet. Use spatula if necessary to release jelly candy from the pan in one piece.

9. Cut into 1-inch cubes by pressing knife down through jelly—do not draw through.

10. Coat squares thoroughly by rolling in granulated or confectioners' sugar. Place on rack to dry overnight.

Store in airtight container. Will stay moist for approximately 2 weeks at room temperature.

The Basic Recipe for these candies will be firm enough for dipping in Chocolate or Summer Coating.

Yield: Twenty-seven 1-inch squares.

Variations:

Mint-Flavored Jelly Candies: Omit fruit juices and rind; substitute ½ cup (120 ml) water and flavor with ¼ teaspoon (1.25 ml) oil of peppermint, wintergreen, or clove. See Coloring and Flavoring Charts (pp. 30-31) for shade of food color or paste appropriate to each flavor.

Turkish Jellies: Omit yellow food coloring, orange juice, and rind. Substitute 4 table-spoons (60 ml) crème de menthe or other mint-flavored liqueur and 6 drops green food coloring.

Turkish Orange Jellies: Omit orange and lemon rind and substitute 4 tablespoons (60 ml) Curaçao or other orange-flavored liqueur and ½ cup (120 ml) candied cherries, finely chopped.

Unmolding and Cutting:

To shape the jellies, use a knife, or any small cutter. A few rules for Jelly Candies:

1. Pour the cooked gelatin mixture into a well-oiled pan.

2. Firm in the refrigerator.

3. Place pan on hot Turkish towel for a few seconds to loosen bottom, if the jellies are difficult to remove.

4. Sugar coat, then let them stand, well separated, in a warm and dry place for several hours or overnight to crust the coating.

5. Store in airtight container at room temperature for approximately 2 weeks or use for immediate gift giving or mailing.

Jelly-Marshmallow Layered Candies

(Not Recommended as Centers for Coating)

Ever wonder how to make those tantalizing delicious jelly squares layered with marsh-mallow? Confectioners' supply houses make the molds and include the how-to

instructions. (See Sources of Supply, p. 218.) Better yet, let's do our own thing!

Preparation:

1. Use any flavor combination. Pour the cooked Jelly Candy mixture into two well-oiled Pyrex loaf pans, 9 x 5 x 3 inches. Place in refrigerator to firm.

2. In the meantime, prepare recipe for *Uncooked Marshmallows* (p. 62).

3. Pour the marshmallow over the firmed jelly candy. Try to keep the layers equal in depth. (Visibility is the reason for using a Pyrex pan.) Firm in the refrigerator overnight.

4. Turn out onto lightly oiled baking sheet. Use spatula if necessary to release candy from the pan in one piece.

5. Cut into 1-inch cubes by pressing knife down through jelly and marshmallow—do not draw through. Or cut into bars about 1 inch wide and 3 inches in length.

6. Dip cubes in confectioners' sugar or granulated sugar. Place on rack to dry over-night.

Store in airtight container. Will stay moist for about 2 weeks.

Yield: Fifty-four 1-inch cubes.

Neapolitan Jellies: Make three layers. Have the bottom layer jelly, the middle marsh-mallow, and the top jelly. Coat as above for layered candies. If the top layer starts to set before it is used, reheat slightly and then pour.

Chapter 7
MARZIPAN

The name marzipan has been used for many centuries for fondant-type candies with a foundation of almond paste. Tradition says such use began when the Crusaders brought the candy back to Europe in the shape of a coin, called the *marchpane*, a word derived from Arabic. The confection became very popular in the sophisticated cities of Venice and Paris.

A century ago, no American Christmas would have been complete without exquisitely shaped and tinted marzipan fruits, vegetables, flowers, and old-fashioned marzipan Christmas-tree ornaments, shaped by hand or in special wooden molds which today are collectors' items. Marzipan sweetmeats are still very much a part of the traditional European Christmas celebration. In Denmark, where marzipan is immensely popular, a molded pink pig is given at Christmas for good luck. These make especially clever party favors.

Marzipan is classified as one of the more expensive varieties of candy because you need 1 ½ cups (360 ml) shelled almonds to make one cup (240 ml) of paste. Filberts or Brazil nuts are acceptable substitutes for the almonds in making the paste. You can also buy good-grade almond paste from bakeries, confectioners' supply houses, and well-stocked supermarket gourmet shelves.

Marzipan can be prepared ahead and stored in an airtight container in the refrigerator for several weeks. Almonds can be ground in a blender or in a food processor until very fine.

For gift giving, place each piece of marzipan in a crinkle cup, then pack in boxes or tins. Then wrap very well. I use freezer bags. These confections may be kept at room temperature for at least 2 weeks. They may be refrigerated for 2 months and frozen for up to 6 months. If refrigerated or frozen, let stand at room temperature for at least 6 hours before removing outside wrapping. Otherwise moisture will form on the candies.

Basic Tinted Marzipan

(Not Recommended as Centers for Coating)

Utensils:

1 large mixing bowl
1 set measuring spoons
1 set measuring cups
1 wooden spoon
1 large baking sheet

Ingredients:

1 cup (240 ml) (8-ounce can or 227 grams) almond paste or use *Blender-Ground Almond Paste* (p. 73)
¼ cup (60 ml) (½ stick) sweet butter, softened
2 tablespoons (30 ml) white kirsch, orange juice, or a few drops of rose water
2 teaspoons (10 ml) corn syrup
¼ teaspoon (1.25 ml) pure almond extract
2½ cups (600 ml) confectioners' sugar, sifted
3 or 4 drops red food coloring
3 or 4 drops green food coloring

Preparation:

1. Combine the almond paste and butter in mixing bowl. Work this mixture with the hands or a wooden spoon until creamy.

2. Add the kirsch, corn syrup, and almond extract. Work until thoroughly mixed.

3. Shape into round ball and divide into three equal portions. Reserve two portions for tinting.

4. Into the white portion sift ¾ cup (180 ml) confectioners' sugar, a small amount at a time, to make a smooth paste.

5. Dust the baking sheet with confectioners' sugar and knead the paste mixture (adding as much confectioners' sugar as needed to keep the marzipan from sticking) until it is firm enough to hold its shape.

6. Wrap in waxed paper or foil and chill in the refrigerator.

7. Color the other two portions, one with the red, the other with the green food coloring (or any other desired shades). See Coloring and Flavoring Charts (pp. 30-31).

8. Sift in confectioners' sugar and knead in the same manner as for white marzipan.

9. Chill in the refrigerator.

Yield: Three portions of white, red, and green marzipan to be molded or used to stuff dried fruits. Enough to stuff approximately 60 dates.

Molding Marzipan

Marzipan, prepared according to the recipes in this book, may be shaped in various ways. Before shaping, wipe hands occasionally with a damp cloth to impart a soft sheen to the candies. Marzipan made with a commercial base dries more quickly than the homemade kind, so it cannot be worked as easily.

There are, of course, many many ways of making and molding marzipan confections. In some cases one needs special tools and molds and a great deal of dexterity. The molding of marzipan is, indeed, a special craft that could fill an entire cookbook. However, this would be mainly of interest to commercial candymakers. If you have the talent for sculpture, the delightful candy trifles are excellent for a round-the-table effort by the whole family. Do your practice work with the uncooked recipe for marzipan potatoes in this section.

Order professional molds from confectioners' supply houses. They come in the shape of hearts, flowers, fruits, vegetables, et cetera, plus a Christmas assortment of bells, holly, star, tree, Santa figure, and Santa's face. Also order plastic stems for the traditional bright-red marzipan strawberries.

If you are using molds, remember to form your marzipan in balls or ovals and roll very lightly in cornstarch, shaking off excess starch before packing into molds. Also dust the molds lightly with cornstarch as you reuse them. Professional molds come with instructions for shaping two-tone candies. Basically they tell the candymaker to divide and color the marzipan to be used. Layer the molds in the desired effect, press down, wipe off surplus, let harden, and then turn out onto waxed paper. Dry before handling.

Glazing and Coloring Marzipan

The majority of marzipan candies are more attractive without glazing, but, if desired, a quick glaze can be made with ½ cup (120 ml) warmed corn syrup mixed with 1 tablespoon (15 ml) hot water and stirred very well to blend.

The marzipan candies must be dried for several hours before glaze is applied and must be dried several more hours before packing and storing. Apply the glaze with a small brush. While painting on the glaze, keep swirling the brush in the mixture to keep it from separating. Do not attempt glazing on a hot and humid day because the glaze will absorb moisture from the air and never lose its sticky surface.

Marzipan to be surface-colored must also stand at room temperature for several hours—depending upon the humidity in the air—to form a glaze before colors are brushed on. Paint the candies with food coloring or paste, using a fine artist's brush with the tip removed. Brush liquid colorings on the finished shapes instead of mixing them with the confection. Dilute the coloring with water until you obtain the desired shade. Order coloring pastes from confectioners' supply houses. I recommend them for the deeper

and more brilliant colors. Refer to Coloring and Flavoring Charts (pp. 30-31).

Hand-Molding Marzipan

Flowers: Hand-mold pale-pink marzipan into small, thin flower petals. Arrange them in the form of small rosebuds. It may be necessary to use a few drops of corn syrup to hold the petals together.

Leaves: Roll out oval shapes of green marzipan and flatten them. Make vein markings in the leaves with the blunt edge of a table knife.

Fruit Baskets: Roll white marzipan out as thin as for pie crust. Cut into 2-inch circles with a fluted cookie cutter. Arrange small tidbits of colorful crystallized fruit on each. Mold each fruit-filled circle into a basket that is oval in shape. Use a thin strip of candied citron or angelica for the handle.

Dipping caramel (p. 98) can be spooned over the crystallized fruit to give the traditional Continental effect. These baskets can be used as cake decorations.

Peapods: Mold flat, oval shapes using white marzipan and put a row of small green balls in the center. Press the edges of the pods together.

Marzipan Rye Bread: Mix marzipan with chopped nuts (any kind), chopped crystallized ginger, and glacé cherries. Shape the mixture into 1 or 2 loaves and brush them with melted semi-sweet chocolate or chocolate coating. Slice to serve.

Marzipan Mushrooms: Make the desired number of mushrooms by first rolling small balls in varying sizes up to 1 inch in diameter so the finished musrooms will be of graduated size. Flatten one side of each ball to shape "mushroom caps." As soon as each cap is formed brush flat underside with cocoa, otherwise the finished marzipan may dry too much to absorb the cocoa. Make mushroom stems by rolling small balls of marzipan into cylindrical shapes. Attach stems to caps with drop of water or corn syrup. Dry for several hours.

Apricots: Use dark-orange paste. Roll marzipan into slightly oval balls. Make a dent with the blunt edge of table knife. Attach small leaf of green marzipan.

Lemons: Use light-yellow paste or coloring. Roll marzipan to resemble small lemons. Roll across small grater to create rough impressions. A whole clove or a chocolate sprinkle may be inserted into the end for a stem.

Strawberries: Use red paste. Shape, and brush each berry lightly with warm corn syrup, then dip and roll around in red sugar sprinkles. Form green marzipan leaf and attach with a drop of corn syrup.

Cherries: Use dark-red paste. Make cherries in pairs by rolling two separate balls and placing them together to dry. Attach green marzipan leaf with small amount corn syrup.

Marzipan Mosaics: For these you will need at least ¾ cup (180 ml) white marzipan plus three separate ¼ cups (60 ml) of marzipan colors—rose, green, and lilac. Use Coloring and Flavoring Charts (pp. 30-31). Form each color into a roll not more than ⅓ inch in diameter. Set aside on waxed paper to firm. Sprinkle a baking sheet with granulated sugar and roll out the white marzipan into a strip 1½ inches wide and as long as the tinted rolls. Place the three tinted rolls, side by side, on the flat strip of white marzipan. Now fold the white edges up around the tinted rolls and seal the edges with a touch of apricot jam. Roll very gently to mold the inside colors together. Set aside on waxed paper to firm or chill in the refrigerator. Cut into slices about ½ inch thick. Sprinkle with granulated sugar, and set aside to dry before storing or gift wrapping.

Yield: Approximately ¾ pound (341 grams).

Marzipan Neapolitans: Color equal portions of marzipan in delicate contrasting shades. Use Coloring and Flavoring Charts (pp. 30-31). Roll out each shade to an identical size. Brush the surface of one very lightly with unbeaten egg white and press a second color on top, using a spatula to lift it in place. Continue layering until all shades are used. The finished slab should not be more than 1 inch thick. Smooth the top very gently with a rolling pin. Set aside on waxed paper to firm, or chill in the refrigerator. Cut into strips 1 inch wide and then into 1-inch cubes. Roll cubes in confectioners' sugar. Arrange in candy dish so the rainbow sides show.

Marzipan Nut Baskets: Roll white or colored marzipan out very thin as for pie crust. Cut small circles with a fluted 1½-inch cookie cutter. Chop any kind of nut rather coarsely. Knead this in a very small quantity of apricot jam—just enough to bind the mixture. In the center of each circle of marzipan place just enough of the nut mixture to allow the fluted edges to be pressed upwards to create a basket effect. Decorate each basket with a piece of crystallized cherry or candied violet.

Marzipan Stuffed Dates: Choose plump dessert dates, and remove the pits carefully. Replace the pits with small rolls of tinted marzipan, leaving the date slightly open so the color shows. Finish by rolling in granulated sugar.

Marzipan Frosted Prunes: In a mixing bowl soak 24 plump, ready-to-eat pitted prunes in 1 cup (240 ml) white kirsch for 2 hours. Drain the prunes thoroughly (reserving the kirsch for another use), and pat them dry on paper towels. Spread the prunes open to form pockets and fill each with a piece of pink, green, or white marzipan large enough to show on the surface. Finish by rolling the prunes in granulated sugar. The marzipan may be decorated with a bit of crystallized cherry or other fruit or nut halves.

Marzipan Cherry Ginger Whirls: Insert a small piece of crystallized ginger in each crystallized cherry. Cut very thin narrow strips of white marzipan and band each cherry so the red shows on top and bottom. Finish by rolling in granulated sugar. Dry on waxed paper.

Dipping Marzipan

In Germany and France most chocolate-coated candies have marzipan cream centers. In England and the Scandinavian countries pieces of marzipan cream dipped in toffee (Caramel Coating) are considered very tasty morsels. The two following are classic European sweetmeats:

Leprechaun Hats: Mold red or green marzipan into ½-inch balls. Dip them into Caramel Coating. Place them on a baking sheet lined with waxed paper to set and glaze over.

Marzipan Toffee: Mold marzipan into ½-inch balls. Dip them into Caramel Coating. Immediately place each warm ball in a foil crinkle cup. (See Sources of Supply, p. 217.) The excess caramel will fill the cup, which the taster peels off before eating.

Blender-Ground Almond Paste

(Recommended as Centers for Chocolate, Summer, Fondant, or Caramel Coating)

If you lack an immediate source of supply, the following recipe produces an excellent almond paste—the basis for marzipan candies.

Utensils:

Blender or food processor
1   set measuring spoons
1   set measuring cups
1   coarse sieve
1   wooden spoon
1   small mixing bowl
1   1-quart saucepan

Ingredients:

1½ cups (360 ml) blanched almonds,
      thoroughly dried but not roasted
¾   cup (180 ml) superfine granulated sugar
1   tablespoon (15 ml) fresh lemon juice
2   tablespoons (30 ml) water
Dash of salt

Preparation:

1. Blender grind ¼ cup (60 ml) almonds.

2. Empty into coarse sieve and return any large pieces to blender container. Continue this process, ¼ cup at a time, until all almonds are finely ground.

3. Combine the sugar, lemon juice, water, and salt in saucepan. Boil for 5 minutes over moderate heat.

4. Remove from heat. Pour over ground almonds and mix well with wooden spoon.

5. Mold into ball.

6. Let age in tightly covered container in refrigerator for at least 4 days.

Yield: Approximately 1¾ cups (420 ml).

Marzipan Potatoes

(Not Recommended as Centers for Coating)

This recipe can be easily managed by at-home candymakers. Let the family help you with this easy-to-make candy. Even the very youngest participant can flatten potatoes into Smile Faces. *Place in a small rough-finished wooden bowl and use for St. Patrick's Day motif.*

Utensils:

Blender or food processor
1   set measuring spoons
1   set measuring cups
1   coarse sieve
1   wooden spoon
1   large mixing bowl

Ingredients:

1 ¼ cups (300 ml) blanched almonds, filberts,
      or Brazil nuts, thoroughly dried but not
      roasted
1   cup (240 ml) confectioners' sugar, sifted
1   egg yolk, well beaten
1   tablespoon (15 ml) butter, melted
1   tablespoon (15 ml) brandy or rum
Cocoa for coating

Preparation:

1. Blender grind ¼ cup (60 ml) nuts.

2. Empty into coarse sieve and return any large pieces to blender container. Continue this process, ¼ cup at a time, until all nuts are finely ground.

3. Combine the nuts, sugar, egg yolk, butter, and brandy in mixing bowl. Work this mixture with the hands until it forms a round ball.

4. Pinch off small pieces about the size of walnuts and with your fingers shape them into slightly oval balls to simulate small potatoes.

5. With a toothpick poke "eyes" in the marzipan potatoes, then coat them well with cocoa.

6. Place on waxed paper and dry for several hours.

Ideal for gift giving.

Yield: Approximately 1 pound (454 grams).

TEMPERATURE-CONTROLLED CANDY

The fundamental principles of temperature-controlled candy-making depend upon both physical and chemical reactions. Most failures in this area of candy-making result from the fact that these reactions are so little understood.

Sugar is the basis of all temperature-controlled candy-making. The crystals of granulated sugar are large and uneven in shape. When dissolved in water and heated, they can be recrystallized into exceedingly small crystals, so smooth and fine they melt on the tongue. Fudge, fondant, or any other cream candy is an example of the recrystallization process. In caramels, brittles, or clear hard candy, crystal formations must be prevented entirely.

All necessary instructions have been carefully written into each recipe for temperature-controlled candies. Following them you will soon find yourself developing the skill to turn out an array of confections far beyond your greatest expectations.

Chapter 8
FUDGE

Soft and creamy, this melt-in-your mouth confection of sugar, butter, and, often, chocolate, is among the most popular of all homemade candies, but one that is very often poorly made. It is said to have originated in the late nineteenth century at one of the Seven Sister Colleges. Whether or not this is true, Janet McKenzie Hill, a well-known cooking authority of her day, gave recipes for Smith, Vassar, and Wellesley fudges in a 1914 pamphlet published by a commercial chocolate firm. It seems that Vassar Fudge was made with granulated sugar and cream; Smith girls preferred brown sugar, molasses, and cream; Wellesley sisters did their thing with marshmallows. Still, even in those days and those places, there must have been as many variations of variations as there were creative sorority sisters! Peanut butter, preserved dried fruits and nuts, different kinds of sweeteners, and pinches of spice are among the many ingredients which today lend their names to different versions of this popular confection.

Here at your fingertips is the guidance needed to make perfect fudge: so soft and creamy that each bite vanishes elegantly in the mouth, so firm and smooth that it cuts into small, clean squares for dipping in Chocolate, Summer, or Caramel Coating, and so professional in overall quality that it establishes you as a fudge-making expert.

Fudge-Making Basics:

Step 1: Lightly grease the sides of the pan before adding the ingredients. This helps to prevent the formation of sugar crystals on the sides of the pan during the cooking process. (See p. 29 for problems relating to crystallization in candy-making.)

Keep calm if the fudge curdles during the cooking process. Curdling simply shows that the acid of the chocolate is reacting properly with the milk.

Step 2: Watch the temperature! Once the boiling point is reached, the mixture becomes very sensitive to jarring, stirring, scraping, or beating, and it increases in sensitiveness as the temperature registers higher on the thermometer. Probably the most important consideration in making good fudge is the temperature of the mixture when beating is begun. Jarring, stirring, or scraping of the syrup before it has cooled to 110°F. (43°C.) will start the formation of sugar crystals, and they will multiply throughout the mass, making the candy coarse and grainy. Attempts to speed cooling generally complicate the procedure, and those for whom time is of the essence would do well to use the *Professional Method.* (see below) or substitute one of the *Quick and Easy* fudge recipes.

Step 3: Fudge goes through interesting changes in appearance during the beating process. It will be glossy and quite thin at first. As the beating continues, the gloss will gradually disappear until, quite suddenly, the mixture starts to thicken. Drop a small quantity from a spoon onto a piece of waxed paper. If it holds its shape, the beating is done. Turn immediately into the greased pan.

Don't be discouraged if your fudge does harden in the pan before you can turn it out.

This can happen to the most accomplished fudgemaker. Just scrape the whole mass onto a baking sheet, as in the *Professional Method,* and knead it, while it is still warm, into a delectable creamy confection.

Step 4: Always prepare the lightly greased pans or molds while the candy is cooling to the temperature recommended for beating. Depending upon the humidity in the air, the candy can firm during the beating process in what will seem to you record time.

Step 5: The fudge should be spread to a depth of ½ to ¾ inch and, when partially cooled, cut into 1-inch squares with a warm knife coated with butter. Squares are traditional; however, this can be varied into diamonds, rectangles, et cetera, for added interest. If the squares are to be dipped in coating, they should be cut into ½-inch pieces.

Professional Fudge Center: Method-Making Basics

This technique for creaming and kneading fudge into soft centers to be dipped in Chocolate, Summer, or Caramel Coating is used by professional chocolatiers. However, my sister first learned of the method from a very elderly lady who remembers these confections from her youth in the rural Midwest.

Any cooked fudge can be "worked" with a spatula as for fondant-making until its color lightens and its texture changes to a soft buttercrème consistency. By following this method, you can eliminate the sudden hardening of the candy mixture in the pan during the beating process. Unfortunately, it also cheats the children out of the time-honored tradition of scraping the candy pan. After the mixture has been "worked" with the spatula it can be kneaded by hand into a pliable consistency suitable for forming

Easter eggs, fudge logs, and other interesting shapes.

Step 1. Assemble baking sheet with sides and wide spatula or fondant paddle (see Sources of Supply, p. 217). Prepare fudge as recipe directs, cooking syrup to recommended soft-ball stage.

Step 2. Quickly run baking sheet under cold-water faucet and shake off excess moisture.

Step 3. Place dampened sheet over the rack for rapid cooling.

Step 4. Holding the saucepan down close to the surface, slowly pour the hot syrup in a steady stream onto the baking sheet, jarring the mixture as little as possible.

Step 5. Do not scrape pan.

Step 6. Add butter to syrup mixture, but do not stir.

Step 7. Cool to lukewarm (10 to 12 minutes). Test by placing the palm of your hand underneath the baking sheet. If it feels only slightly warm, the mixture is ready to be worked with a spatula.

Step 8. Add flavoring. Cream as for making Fondant.

Step 9. Shape into a rectangle and cut into squares with large knife, or knead into desired shapes, or press into lightly greased molds.

Ingredients and Substitutions:

Butter adds its own rich creamy flavor to fudge, but you can substitute other mild-tasting vegetable fat if your recipe is already rich in chocolate, brown sugar, or molasses.

Chocolate squares can be replaced. Use 3 tablespoons (45 ml) butter or margarine for each 1-ounce (28-gram) square of unsweetened chocolate.

Corn syrup retards the thickening of cooked candy syrup and helps prevent graininess. However, fudges made with corn syrup require longer beating. Light corn syrup (dark corn syrup is rarely used in candy-making) can be replaced, you may use ½ teaspoon (2.5 ml) lemon juice for each 2 cups of sugar called for in the recipe. I ordinarily do not use cream of tartar as a substitute for corn syrup because the professionals consider this ingredient rather "treacherous" —the reason being that some water supplies contain free alkali, which will neutralize the cream of tartar.

Instant nonfat dry milk may be reconstituted and used to replace whole milk. However, unless one tablespoon (15 ml) of butter or margarine is added to each ½ cup (120 ml) of milk as reconstituted, the fudge will be less rich and nutritious than that made with whole milk.

Shaping Fudge:

Fudge—after it has been shaped into a rectangle about ½ inch in depth on the baking sheet, and before it becomes hard— can be cut into many creative shapes. Slightly warm fudge will remain creamy long enough to be coiled, twisted, rolled, or pressed into lightly greased molds.

Fudge Hearts, Rounds, Chocolate Babies, or Other Small Forms: Prepare the fudge and shape into a rectangle about ½ inch in depth. Lightly grease cutter and carefully cut through fudge to form shape as in cutting out cookie dough. These forms can be coated with Chocolate or Summer Coating, or left plain to be decorated by pastry tube with a motif appropriate for a particular occasion.

Fudge Marbles: Prepare the fudge and shape into a rectangle about ½ inch in depth. Divide the rectangle in half and shape into two long rolls about ½ inch in diameter. Pinch or cut off small pieces and roll into smooth balls. If you like, roll in finely grated coconut or chopped nuts to add pretty texture and color to a candy-box assortment.

Fudge-Covered Dates: Cut dates in half lengthwise; remove the pits. Prepare fudge as for the marbles above. Flatten the marble and wrap around the date half.

Layered Fudge: Prepare any two fudge recipes, using compatible flavors. Chocolate and caramel or pastel-tinted fruit flavors make especially tasty combinations. Shape the two flavors into equal-size rectangles about ⅓ inch in depth. As soon as the second flavor has been shaped, and while it is still warm, press it firmly onto the first flavor to form the two layers. Cut into 1-inch squares. Wipe the knife with a paper towel after each cutting to keep the colors from smearing together on the edges.

Dipping Fudge:

The firmness of fudge makes it one of the best candies for a novice to use in a first attempt at dipping. Prepare and shape, cut or mold fudge as described on pp. 78-79. Store in airtight container, separating layers with waxed paper, at least 24 hours ahead of dipping time, to "ripen" the flavor. Or freeze the fudge to be dipped and bring to room temperature before dipping.

Almost any fudge-type confection can be used for dipping except pralines, which are likely to be too large for individual pieces of candy.

Basic Chocolate Fudge

(Recommended as Centers for Chocolate, Summer, or Caramel Coating)

Utensils:

1   2-quart heavy saucepan
1   wooden spoon
1   set measuring spoons
1   set measuring cups
Candy thermometer
1   square pan, 8 x 8 x 2 inches

Ingredients:

2   squares (2 ounces or 57 grams) unsweetened chocolate, chopped
⅔   cup (160 ml) milk or light (coffee) cream
2   cups (480 ml) granulated sugar, sifted
2   tablespoons (30 ml) light corn syrup
⅛   teaspoon (.6 ml) salt
2   tablespoons (30 ml) butter
1   teaspoon (5 ml) vanilla

Preparation:

1. Lightly grease sides of saucepan.

2. Add chocolate and milk. Cook over low heat, stirring constantly until mixture is smooth.

3. Stir in sugar, corn syrup, and salt. Continue stirring with the wooden spoon, over low heat until sugar is dissolved. You should not be able to feel sugar grains when you rub the spoon against the sides of the saucepan.

4. Remove from heat and, with a damp paper towel or small sponge, wipe sugar grains from the sides of the pan above the liquid level.

5. Start the syrup boiling and clip on the candy thermometer.

6. Cook over medium heat, without stirring, until thermometer registers 238°F. or 114°C. (syrup forms a soft ball (p. 26) in cold water).

7. Remove from heat and add butter. Cool, without stirring, to lukewarm (110°F. or 43°C.).

8. Add vanilla and beat vigorously with wooden spoon until mixture begins to thicken and lose its gloss.

9. Quickly spread into lightly greased pan. Cool until firm.

10. Cut into 1-inch squares.

Yield: 64 pieces.

Variations:

Chocolate Fruit or Nut Fudge: One-half (120 ml) to 1 cup (240 ml) of chopped dried fruit such as dates, figs, raisins, or candied cherries may be added to Basic Recipe. To make Nut Fudge use unsalted chopped nuts alone or in combination with dried diced fruit. Unsalted almonds, filberts, peanuts, pecans, hickory nuts, or walnuts are nice. Lightly roasting all but the pecans, hickory nuts, and walnuts improves the flavor of the finished product. Stir in the chopped fruit or nuts just as the mixture begins to thicken and lose its gloss.

Chocolate Coconut Fudge: Add fresh or commercially prepared shredded coconut to Basic Recipe. If fresh coconut is used, be sure it is thoroughly dried before combining it with the candy or it will make the fudge too soft. Fresh coconut can be dried by placing on a baking sheet in a very slow oven for a few minutes. Stir in ½ cup (120 ml) to 1 cup

(240 ml) just as mixture begins to thicken and lose its gloss.

Marshmallow Fudge: Add 1 cup (240 ml) diced marshmallows when adding butter in Basic Recipe. Do not stir until mixture has cooled to lukewarm (110°F. or 43°C.).

Chocolate Peanut Butter Fudge: Substitute ¼ cup (60 ml) peanut butter for the butter in Basic Recipe. Do not stir until mixture has cooled to lukewarm (110°F. or 43°C.).

Super Fudge

(Recommended as Centers for Chocolate Coating)

This easy recipe for fudge is made with dried milk solids. Delicious plain, it is also excellent when molded into ½-inch balls and used as the rich centers of chocolate-coated French creams.

Utensils:

1   3-quart heavy saucepan
1   wooden spoon
1   set measuring spoons
1   set measuring cups
Candy thermometer
1   square pan, 8 x 8 x 2 inches

Ingredients:

¼   cup (60 ml) butter
1½ cups (360 ml) boiling water
3   cups (720 ml) granulated sugar, sifted
⅔   cup (160 ml) cocoa, preferably Dutch
2   teaspoons (10 ml) light corn syrup
⅓   cup (80 ml) instant nonfat dry milk solids
1   teaspoon (5 ml) vanilla

Preparation:

1. Melt butter in saucepan over low heat.

2. Add boiling water and stir until well blended.

3. Add sugar, cocoa, and corn syrup. Continue stirring with the wooden spoon, over low heat until sugar is dissolved. You should not be able to feel sugar grains when you rub the spoon against the sides of the saucepan.

4. Remove from heat and, with a damp paper towel or small sponge, wipe sugar grains from the sides of the pan above the liquid level.

5. Start the syrup boiling and clip on the candy thermometer.

6. Cook over medium heat, without stirring, until thermometer registers 236°F. or 113°C. (syrup forms a soft ball (p. 26) in cold water).

7. Remove from heat; without stirring, cool to lukewarm (110°F. or 43°C.).

8. Add milk solids and vanilla and beat vigorously with wooden spoon until mixture begins to thicken and lose its gloss.

9. Quickly spread into lightly greased pan. Cool until firm.

10. Cut into 1-inch squares.

Yield: 64 pieces.

Variation:

Jamaican Fudge: Substitute 1½ cups (360 ml) boiling hot strong coffee for the boiling water. Substitute ¾ teaspoon (3.75 ml) ground cinnamon for the vanilla. Shape into ½-inch balls. Luscious when dipped in Caramel Coating!

Chocolate Molasses Fudge

(Not Recommended as Centers for Coating)
A high-style, extra-rich fudge.

Utensils:

1   2-quart heavy saucepan
1   wooden spoon
1   set measuring spoons
1   set measuring cups
Candy thermometer
1   square pan, 8 x 8 x 2 inches

Ingredients:

1   cup (240 ml) granulated sugar, sifted
1   cup (240 ml) light brown sugar, firmly packed
¼   cup (60 ml) light molasses
½   cup (120 ml) light (coffee) cream
2   squares (2 ounces or 57 grams) unsweetened chocolate, chopped
¼   cup (60 ml) butter
1½ teaspoons (7.5 ml) vanilla

Preparation:

1. Lightly grease sides of saucepan.

2. Add the two sugars, molasses, cream, and chocolate.

3. Cook over low heat, stirring constantly with the wooden spoon, until sugar is dissolved. You should not be able to feel sugar grains when you rub the spoon against the sides of the saucepan.

4. Remove from heat and, with a damp paper towel or small sponge, wipe sugar grains from the sides of the pan above the liquid level.

5. Start the syrup boiling and clip on the candy thermometer.

6. Cook over medium heat, stirring occasionally to prevent mixture from scorching, until thermometer registers 238°F. or 114°C. (syrup forms a soft ball (p. 26) in cold water).

7. Remove from heat; add butter and, without stirring, cool to lukewarm (110°F. or 43°C.).

8. Add vanilla and beat vigorously with wooden spoon until mixture begins to thicken and lose its gloss.

9. Quickly spread into lightly greased pan. Cool until firm.

10. Cut into 1-inch squares.

Yield: 64 pieces.

Chocolate Pecan Marshmallow Fudge

(Not Recommended as Centers for Coating)

The following fudge recipe will delight lovers of sour cream, which adds a rich flavor that somehow seems just right—not too sweet and not too tart.

Utensils:

1   2-quart heavy saucepan
1   wooden spoon
1   set measuring spoons
1   set measuring cups
Candy thermometer
1   square pan, 8 x 8 x 2 inches

Ingredients:

2   cups (480 ml) granulated sugar, sifted
1   cup (240 ml) commercial sour cream
2   squares (2 ounces or 57 grams)
      unsweetened chocolate, chopped
½   teaspoon (2.5 ml) salt
1   teaspoon (5 ml) vanilla
1   cup (240 ml) pecans, chopped
1   cup (240 ml) miniature marshmallows

Preparation:

1. Lightly grease sides of saucepan.

2. Add sugar, sour cream, chocolate, and salt.

3. Cook over low heat, stirring constantly with the wooden spoon, until sugar is dissolved. You should not be able to feel sugar grains when you rub the spoon against the sides of the saucepan.

4. Remove from heat and, with a damp paper towel or small sponge, wipe sugar grains from the sides of the pan above the liquid level.

5. Start the syrup boiling and clip on the candy thermometer.

6. Cook over medium heat, stirring occasionally to prevent mixture from scorching, until the thermometer registers 238°F. or 114°C. (syrup forms a soft ball (p. 26) in cold water.

7. Remove from heat and, without stirring, cool to lukewarm (110°F. or 43°C.).

8. Add vanilla and beat vigorously with wooden spoon until mixture begins to thicken and lose its gloss.

9. Immediately stir in the pecans and marshmallows. The marshmallows should remain rather firm and not melt into the fudge.

10. Quickly spread into lightly greased pan. Cool until firm.

11. Cut into 1-inch squares.

Yield: 64 pieces.

Black Walnut Stretched Fudge

(Recommended as Centers for Chocolate or Caramel Coating)

Native American black walnuts have a very special taste which some people find too strong in flavor. If that means you or your candy eaters, substitute the milder English or California walnuts.

This is a very old recipe from my family; we call it Stretched Fudge *because it is "worked" with a spatula as in the* Professional Method, pp. 78-79.

Utensils:

1   4-quart heavy saucepan
1   wooden spoon
1   set measuring spoons
1   set measuring cups
Candy thermometer
1   spatula, 3 to 5 inches wide
1   large baking sheet with sides

Ingredients:

4   cups (960 ml) granulated sugar, sifted
2¼ cups (540 ml) heavy (whipping) cream
1   tablespoon (15 ml) light corn syrup
4   squares (4 ounces or 114 grams)
    unsweetened chocolate, chopped
¼   teaspoon (1.25 ml) salt
1   tablespoon (15 ml) vanilla
1   cup (240 ml) black walnuts, chopped

Preparation:

1. Lightly grease sides of saucepan.

2. Add sugar, cream, corn syrup, chocolate, and salt.

3. Cook over low heat, stirring constantly with the wooden spoon, until sugar is dissolved. You should not be able to feel sugar grains when you rub the spoon against the sides of the saucepan.

4. Remove from heat and, with a damp paper towel or small sponge, wipe sugar grains from the sides of the pan above the liquid level.

5. Start the syrup boiling and clip on the candy thermometer.

6. Cook over medium heat, stirring occasionally to prevent mixture from scorching, until the thermometer registers 236°F. or 113°C. (syrup forms a soft ball (p. 26) in cold water).

7. Remove from heat and, without stirring, cool to lukewarm (110°F. or 43°C.).

8. Turn out onto lightly greased baking sheet.

9. Add vanilla and walnuts.

10. Begin to "work" the fudge with a spatula in a back-and-forth motion as in the *Professional Method*, pp. 78-79.

11. After the candy has firmed into a creamy mass, form a long roll and slice to desired thickness.

These rounds are especially nice dipped in Chocolate Coating.

Yield: 2½ pounds (1136 grams).

Velvet Fudge

(Not Recommended as Centers for Coating)

This recipe was given to me by Madeline Willett Raab, former Base Manager of In-Flight Services for Eastern Airlines at Newark Airport. "The texture is perfection." Originally published in "A collection of favorite Bourbon recipes handed down through three generations of the Willett Family of Bardstown, Nelson County, Kentucky. . . heart of the world's most renowned Bourbon country." Perfect for gift giving because the candies pack and ship very well if wrapped individually in foil or waxed paper.

Utensils:

1   2-quart heavy saucepan
1   wooden spoon
1   set measuring spoons
1   set measuring cups
Candy thermometer
Waxed paper

Ingredients:

2   cups (480 ml) granulated sugar, sifted
6   tablespoons (90 ml) cocoa
¾   cup (180 ml) cold water
½   cup (120 ml) butter or margarine
½   teaspoon (2.5 ml) almond extract
2   tablespoons (30 ml) bourbon
Nuts (optional)

Preparation:

1. Lightly grease sides of saucepan.

2. Add sugar, cocoa, water, and butter.

3. Cook over low heat, stirring constantly with the wooden spoon, until mixture is smooth and sugar is dissolved. You should not be able to feel sugar grains when you rub the spoon against the sides of the saucepan.

4. Remove from heat and, with a damp paper towel or small sponge, wipe sugar grains from the sides of the pan above the liquid level.

5. Start the syrup boiling and clip on the candy thermometer.
Warning: Cook slowly after mixture starts to boil, and do not stir during the cooking process, until thermometer registers 234°F. or 112°C. (syrup forms a very soft ball (p. 26) in cold water).

6. Remove from heat and, without stirring, cool to lukewarm (110°F. or 43°C.).

7. Add almond extract and bourbon and beat vigorously with wooden spoon until mixture begins to thicken and lose its gloss.

8. Quickly drop by teaspoonfuls onto waxed paper and top with your favorite nuts if you like.

Yield: Approximately sixty-four 1-inch candies.

Cranbury Fudge

(Recommended as Centers for Chocolate, Summer, or Caramel Coating)
In years past this quantity recipe was prepared and sold by the good ladies of Cranbury, New Jersey, at the annual Princeton Hospital Fête.

Utensils:

1	4-quart heavy saucepan
1	wooden spoon
1	set measuring spoons
1	set measuring cups
Candy thermometer	
1	pan, 11 x 16 x 1 inches

Ingredients:

5	cups (1200 ml) granulated sugar, sifted
½	cup (120 ml) or 1 stick of butter
⅛	teaspoon (.6 ml) salt
1⅔	cups (400 ml) evaporated milk (undiluted)
3	cups (720 ml) semisweet chocolate bits
2½	cups (600 ml) marshmallow crème (7½ or 8 oz. jar)
1	teaspoon (5 ml) vanilla

Preparation:

1. Lightly grease sides of saucepan.

2. Add sugar, butter, salt, and evaporated milk.

3. Stirring constantly, cook over medium heat until sugar is dissolved. You should not be able to feel sugar grains when you rub the wooden spoon against the sides of the saucepan.

4. Remove from heat and, with a damp paper towel or small sponge, wipe sugar grains from the sides of the pan above the liquid level.

5. Start the syrup boiling and clip on the candy thermometer.

6. Cook over medium heat, stirring constantly, until thermometer registers 236°F. or 113°C. (Syrup forms a soft ball (p. 26) in cold water.)

7. Remove from heat and immediately add chocolate bits, marshmallow creme, and vanilla.

8. Stir vigorously until chocolate is melted and all ingredients are well blended.

9. Just as the mixture starts to thicken, turn into lightly greased broiler pan. Cool until firm.

10. Cut into 1-inch squares.

Yield: 4 pounds (1818 grams).

Note: For fund raising the fudge is divided equally to fit in four one-pound boxes. First wrap each 1-pound portion in plastic wrap, then place in individual boxes. Label each box.

White Fudge

(Recommended as Centers for Chocolate, Summer, Fondant or Caramel Coating)

There is very little difference between the basic recipes for white and chocolate fudge in this book. However, the white fudge is a basis for an endless variety of flavors and can be tinted to complement any party color scheme or to add gaiety to a gift-box assortment. I also like to use the fruit flavors for Easter-egg centers to be dipped in Chocolate or Summer Coating.

Utensils:

1   2-quart heavy saucepan
1   wooden spoon
1   set measuring spoons
1   set measuring cups
Candy thermometer
1   square pan, 8 x 8 x 2 inches

Ingredients:

2   cups (480 ml) granulated sugar, sifted
2   tablespoons (30 ml) light corn syrup
⅛   teaspoon (.6 ml) salt
½   cup (120 ml) milk or light (coffee) cream
2   tablespoons (30 ml) butter
1   teaspoon (5 ml) vanilla

Preparation:

1. Lightly grease sides of saucepan.

2. Add sugar, corn syrup, salt, and milk.

3. Cook over low heat, stirring constantly with the wooden spoon, until sugar is dissolved. You should not be able to feel sugar grains when you rub the spoon against the sides of the saucepan.

4. Remove from heat and, with a damp paper towel or small sponge, wipe sugar grains from the sides of the pan above the liquid level.

5. Start the syrup boiling and clip on the candy thermometer.

6. Cook over medium heat, without stirring, until thermometer registers 236°F. or 113°C. (syrup forms a soft ball (p. 26) in cold water).

7. Remove from heat; add butter and, without stirring, cool to lukewarm (110°F. or 43°C.).

8. Add vanilla and beat vigorously with wooden spoon until mixture begins to thicken and lose its gloss.

9. Quickly spread into lightly greased pan. Cool until firm.

10. Cut into 1-inch squares.

Yield: 64 pieces.

Variations:

Pink Coconut Fudge: During beating stir in red food coloring, one drop at a time, until desired shade is obtained. Add 1 cup (240 ml) shredded dried coconut just as mixture begins to thicken and lose its gloss.

Banana Fudge: Omit vanilla and substitute 1 teaspoon (5 ml) banana extract. Add ½ cup (120 ml) finely chopped nuts, if desired. Tint pale yellow.

Cherry Fudge: Omit vanilla and substitute 1 teaspoon (5 ml) cherry extract. Add ½ cup (120 ml) finely chopped candied cherries just as mixture begins to thicken and lose its gloss.

Lemon Fudge: Omit vanilla and substitute 1½ teaspoons (7.5 ml) lemon extract. Tint pale yellow.

Orange Fudge: Omit vanilla and substitute 1 teaspoon (5 ml) orange extract. Tint with 1 drop red and 3 drops yellow food coloring to obtain the desired shade.

Pineapple Fudge: Omit vanilla and substitute 1 teaspoon (5 ml) pineapple extract. Add ½ cup (120 ml) finely chopped candied pineapple just as mixture begins to thicken and lose its gloss.

Raspberry Fudge: Omit vanilla and substitute 1 teaspoon (5 ml) raspberry extract. Tint with 8 drops red and 1 drop blue food coloring to obtain the desired shade.

Rum-Raisin Fudge: Omit vanilla and add 2 tablespoons (30 ml) dark rum. Add ½ cup (120 ml) dry raisins just as mixture begins to thicken and lose its gloss.

Boston Creams: Use light (coffee) cream instead of milk. Add 1 tablespoon (15 ml) freshly grated orange or lemon rind just as mixture begins to thicken and lose its gloss.

White Satin Christmas Fudge

(Not Recommended as Centers for Coating)

Utensils:

1   4-quart heavy saucepan
1   wooden spoon
1   set measuring spoons
1   set measuring cups
Candy thermometer
1   pan, 9 x 12 x 2 inches

Ingredients:

4   cups (960 ml) granulated sugar, sifted
½   cup (120 ml) light corn syrup
½   cup (120 ml) butter
1   cup (240 ml) light (coffee) cream
½   cup (120 ml) water
1   teaspoon (5 ml) salt
2   teaspoons (10 ml) vanilla or 2 tablespoons (30 ml) dark rum
½   cup (120 ml) marshmallow crème
½   cup (120 ml) each of red and green candied cherries, chopped
½   cup (120 ml) pecan or walnut halves

Preparation:

1. Lightly grease sides of saucepan.

2. Add sugar, corn syrup, butter, cream, water, and salt. Cook over low heat, stirring constantly with the wooden spoon, until sugar is dissolved. You should not be able to feel sugar grains when you rub the spoon against the sides of the saucepan.

3. Remove from heat and, with a damp paper towel or small sponge, wipe sugar grains from the sides of the pan above the liquid level.

4. Start the syrup boiling and clip on the candy thermometer.

5. Cook over medium heat, stirring occasionally, until thermometer registers 238°F. or 114°C. (syrup forms a soft ball (p. 26) in cold water).

6. Remove from heat and, without stirring, cool to lukewarm (110°F. or 43°C).

7. Add vanilla and beat vigorously with wooden spoon for a few minutes.

8. Fold in marshmallow crème and continue beating until mixture begins to thicken and lose its gloss.

9. Quickly stir in cherries and nuts and spread into lightly greased pan. Cool until firm.

10. Cut into 1-inch squares.

Yield: 108 pieces.

Old-Fashioned Peanut-Butter Fudge

(Recommended as Centers for Chocolate or Caramel Coating)

No need to be fussy about dissolving sugar grains in this recipe. All the rich ingredients will prevent them from forming in the first place. This is the way this candy used to taste before manufacturers started adding preservatives. My friends are especially fond of my chocolates when I use this mouth-watering recipe to make the centers.

Utensils:

1   2-quart heavy saucepan
1   wooden spoon
1   set measuring spoons
1   set measuring cups
Candy thermometer
1   pan, 8 x 8 x 2 inches

Ingredients:

2   cups (480 ml) granulated sugar, sifted
2   tablespoons (30 ml) light corn syrup
½   cup (120 ml) water
¼   teaspoon (1.25 ml) salt
2   tablespoons (30 ml) butter
2   tablespoons (30 ml) half and half
⅓   cup (80 ml) creamy peanut butter

Preparation:

1. Lightly grease sides of saucepan.

2. Add sugar, corn syrup, water, salt, butter, and half and half. Cook over medium heat, stirring constantly until mixture boils.

3. Clip on candy thermometer and continue cooking, stirring occasionally, until thermometer registers 238°F. or 114°C. (syrup forms a soft ball (p. 26) in cold water).

4. Remove from heat; add peanut butter but do not stir. Cool to lukewarm (110°F. or 43°C.).

5. Beat vigorously with wooden spoon until mixture begins to thicken and lose its gloss.

6. Quickly spread into lightly greased pan. Cool until firm.

7. Cut into 1-inch squares, or for dipping in chocolate, cut into ½-inch squares, or smaller.

Yield: Sixty-four 1-inch pieces.

Maple Cream Candy

(Recommended as Centers for Chocolate or Summer Coating)

Old recipe books in the South refer to maple fudge as "tree molasses candy" because the maple tree was the source of its sweetening, which was maple sap boiled down to a syrup. Gift-wrap these candies in a small wooden bucket or mixing bowl to preserve the memory of that long-ago name. I give them a modern touch by dipping them in rich Chocolate Coating.

Utensils:

1   2-quart heavy saucepan
1   wooden spoon
1   set measuring spoons
1   set measuring cups
Candy thermometer
1   pan, 8 x 8 x 2 inches

Ingredients:

1   cup (240 ml) pure maple syrup
2   cups (480 ml) granulated sugar, sifted
1   cup (240 ml) light (coffee) cream
2   tablespoons (30 ml) light corn syrup
1   cup (240 ml) nuts, any kind, chopped

Preparation:

1. Lightly grease sides of saucepan.

2. Add maple syrup, sugar, cream, and corn syrup. Cook over low heat, stirring constantly until sugar is dissolved. You should not be able to feel sugar grains when you rub the wooden spoon against the sides of the saucepan.

3. Remove from heat and, with a damp paper towel or small sponge, wipe sugar grains from the sides of the pan above the liquid level.

4. Start the syrup boiling and clip on the candy thermometer. Cook over medium heat, without stirring, until thermometer registers 236°F. or 113°C. (syrup forms a soft ball (p. 26) in cold water).

5. Remove from heat and, without stirring, cool to lukewarm (110°F. or 43°C.).

6. Beat vigorously with wooden spoon until mixture begins to thicken and lose its gloss. Quickly add nuts.

7. Quickly spread into lightly greased pan. Cool until firm.

8. Cut into 1-inch squares or, for dipping in chocolate, cut into ½-inch squares.

Yield: Sixty-four 1-inch pieces.

Variation:

Molded Maple Cream Candies: Omit nuts and prepare as in the *Professional Method,* pp. 78-79. Mold into desired shapes.

Basic Old-Fashioned Penuche

(Recommended as Centers for Chocolate or Summer Coating)

Back in the 1700's, the new American colonies imported no less than fifteen grades of soft sugar, ranging in color from white to yellow to brown. The soft sugar we use in this recipe is certainly one the colonists knew: light brown, with the mild brown-sugar flavor just right for penuche.

There are as many different versions of penuche as there are pronunciations and spellings (panocha, penocha, penoche, penuchi). After I started my world travels, I learned that the name is derived from the Mexican-Spanish word for raw sugar and in candy-making refers to a fudge made with brown sugar, butter, cream or milk, and nuts. My Grandmother Heavin made huge platters of what she called Brown-Sugar Fudge; it was a classic penuche.

Utensils:

1   3-quart heavy saucepan
1   wooden spoon
1   set measuring spoons
1   set measuring cups
Candy thermometer
1   square pan, 9 x 9 x 2 inches

Ingredients:

3   cups (720 ml) light brown sugar, firmly packed
1   cup (240 ml) milk or light (coffee) cream
2   tablespoons (30 ml) butter
1   teaspoon (5 ml) vanilla
1   cup (240 ml) walnuts, pecans, or hickory nuts, chopped

Preparation:

1. Lightly grease sides of saucepan.

2. Add sugar and milk. Cook over low heat, stirring constantly with the wooden spoon, until sugar is dissolved. You should not be able to feel sugar grains when you rub the spoon against the sides of the saucepan.

3. Remove from heat and, with a damp paper towel or small sponge, wipe sugar grains from the sides of the pan above the liquid level.

4. Start the syrup boiling and clip on the candy thermometer.

5. Cook over medium heat, without stirring, until thermometer registers 238°F. or 114°C. (syrup forms a soft ball (p. 26) in cold water).

6. Remove from heat; add butter and, without stirring, cool to lukewarm (110°F. or 43°C.).

7. Add vanilla and beat vigorously with wooden spoon until mixture begins to thicken and lose its gloss.

8. Stir in nuts and quickly spread into lightly greased pan. Cool until firm.

9. Cut into 1-inch squares.

Yield: 81 pieces.

Variations:

Coconut Penuche: Around the mountain regions of Kentucky and Tennessee this recipe is also called "Sauerkraut Candy," because pioneer candymakers grated the coconut meat on the sauerkraut cutter. Prepare Basic Recipe, but omit nuts. Substitute 1½ cups (360 ml) shredded or grated dry coconut. If fresh coconut is used, dry it in a slow oven before combining with the candy or it will make the confection too soft.

Mexican Orange Candy: Add 4 tablespoons (60 ml) (2 large oranges) freshly grated orange rind along with the vanilla. Use pecans for traditional flavor.

Creole Pralines

(Not Recommended as Centers for Coating)

Living for two years in the heart of the French Quarter in Old New Orleans, I learned how to make an authentic praline.

Pralines were supposedly named for the French diplomat Caesar du Plessis-Praslin. It is said the Praslin's butler advised him that almonds coated with sugar would not cause indigestion. In the early days the French Creoles in New Orleans substituted native pecans for almonds and made pralines their own confection.

Pralines are made from a fudge mixture which is beaten as soon as it is removed from the heat and dropped like cookie dough into round patties about 2 to 3 inches in diameter. These are the type sold on practically every street corner in the Quarter and bought mostly by tourists.

Utensils:

1   2-quart heavy saucepan
1   wooden spoon
1   set measuring spoons
1   set measuring cups
Candy thermometer
1   large baking sheet

Ingredients:

1   cup (240 ml) light brown sugar, firmly packed
1   cup (240 ml) granulated sugar, sifted
½   cup (120 ml) water or light (coffee) cream
2   tablespoons (30 ml) butter
1   cup (240 ml) pecan halves

Preparation:

1. Lightly grease sides of saucepan.

2. Add the two sugars and water or cream.

(The cream will produce a softer confection.) Cook over low heat, stirring constantly with the wooden spoon, until sugar is dissolved. (You don't want to start the graining reaction of the sugar too soon.) You should not be able to feel sugar grains when you rub the spoon against the sides of the saucepan.

3. Remove from heat and, with a damp paper towel or small sponge, wipe sugar grains from the sides of the pan above the liquid level.

4. Start the syrup boiling and clip on candy thermometer.

5. Cook over medium heat, without stirring, until the thermometer registers 236°F. or 113°C. (syrup forms a soft ball (p. 26) in cold water).

6. Remove from heat and add butter and pecans. Immediately start beating with a wooden spoon and continue until the mixture is just slightly thick and begins to look cloudy. Do not over-beat or the pralines will not spread.

7. Quickly drop by heaping tablespoons onto lightly greased baking sheet. Cool until firm.

Yield: About 24 pieces.

Variations:

Black Walnut Pralines: Omit pecans and substitute 2 cups (480 ml) coarsely chopped black walnuts.

Sherry-Flavored Pralines: Add 1 tablespoon (15 ml) fine Spanish sherry just before pralines are to be dropped.

Maple-Flavored Pralines: Omit granulated sugar and use 2 cups of light brown sugar. Add ½ teaspoon (2.5 ml) maple flavoring just before pralines are to be dropped.

Vanilla Cream Pralines: Omit brown sugar and use 2 cups granulated sugar. Add 1 teaspoon (5 ml) vanilla just before pralines are to be dropped.

Buttermilk Pralines

(Not Recommended as Centers for Coating)

Disregard all rules when you make candies with buttermilk and soda! The soda is not used to make the syrup porous as for a brittle, but to counteract the acidity of the buttermilk. Hence, a word of warning. Use a very large saucepan for this cooking venture. (I use my large soup kettle.) The foaming action of the boiling buttermilk and soda is enough to intimidate the most experienced cook.

If you beat the mixture while it is still hot, it becomes a slightly grainy New Orleans-type praline. Southern candymakers also cool the syrup to lukewarm and beat as for any other fudge. This variation makes my most-requested centers for chocolate dipping. Do not attempt to double this recipe because of the excessive foaming. And don't stray too far from the stove while you are cooking: this is a rather quick-do candy.

Utensils:

1   4-quart heavy saucepan
1   wooden spoon
1   set measuring spoons
1   set measuring cups
Candy thermometer
1   large baking sheet

Ingredients:

2   cups (480 ml) granulated sugar, sifted
1   teaspoon (5 ml) baking soda
⅛   teaspoon (.6 ml) salt
1   cup (240 ml) buttermilk
2   tablespoons (30 ml) butter
2   cups (480 ml) walnut, hickory nuts, or
      pecan halves
1   teaspoon (5 ml) vanilla

Preparation:

1. Lightly grease sides of saucepan.

2. Add sugar, baking soda, salt, and buttermilk. Cook over low heat, stirring constantly with the wooden spoon, until sugar is dissolved. Add butter just before mixture comes to a boil. You should not be able to feel sugar grains when you rub the spoon against the sides of the saucepan.

3. Remove from heat and, with a damp paper towel or small sponge, wipe sugar grains from the sides of the pan above the liquid level.

4. Start the syrup boiling and clip on candy thermometer.

5. Cook over medium-low heat, stirring often, until thermometer registers 236°F. or 113°C. (syrup forms a soft ball (p. 26) in cold water).

6. Remove from heat and add nut halves. Immediately start beating with a wooden spoon and continue until the mixture is just slightly thick and begins to look cloudy. Add vanilla. Do not over-beat or the pralines will not spread.

7. Quickly drop by heaping tablespoons onto lightly greased baking sheet. Cool until firm.

Yield: About 14 pieces.

Variation:

Buttermilk Fudge: *(Recommended as Centers for Chocolate Coating).* Remove syrup from heat at 236°F. or 113°C.; add butter and cool, without stirring, to lukewarm (110°F. or 43°C.). Add vanilla and beat vigorously with wooden spoon until mixture begins to thicken and lose its gloss. Stir in nuts. The nuts are optional; however, it makes a smoother-finished coated chocolate if they are chopped. Quickly spread into lightly greased 8 x 8 x 2 inch pan. Cool until firm. Cut into ½-inch squares for dipping in Chocolate Coating.

Opera Creams

(Recommended as Centers for Chocolate Coating)

Opera Creams have all but disappeared because of the expense involved in hand-dipping these tiny morsels. Originally they were created for operagoers during the Victorian era when it was considered indelicate to be seen chewing in public. It was assumed one could discreetly put one of these dainty chocolate-coated fudge creams into the mouth without being obvious.

"Operas" have excellent keeping qualities because of the large amount of fat in the heavy cream. They can be prepared several weeks before they are to be used, which makes them especially good for storing and shipping.

Utensils:

1   2-quart heavy saucepan
1   wooden spoon
1   set measuring spoons
1   set measuring cups
Candy thermometer
Flat surface for kneading

Ingredients:

2   cups (480 ml) granulated sugar, sifted,
    or 1 cup (240 ml) granulated, sifted, and
    1 cup (240 ml) light brown sugar,
    firmly packed
1   cup (240 ml) milk
¾   cup (180 ml) heavy (whipping) cream
1   tablespoon (15 ml) light corn syrup
⅛   teaspoon (.6 ml) salt
1   teaspoon (5 ml) vanilla
1   cup (240 ml) pecans, chopped

Preparation:

1. Lightly grease sides of saucepan.

2. Add sugar, milk, cream, corn syrup, and salt. Cook over low heat, stirring constantly with the wooden spoon, until sugar is dissolved. You should not be able to feel sugar grains when you rub the spoon against the sides of the saucepan.

3. Start the syrup boiling and clip on the candy thermometer. Cook over medium-low heat, stirring occasionally to keep mixture from scorching, until thermometer registers 236°F. or 113°C. (syrup forms a soft ball (p. 26) in cold water).

4. Remove from heat and, without stirring, cool to lukewarm (110°F. or 43°C.).

5. Add vanilla and beat vigorously with wooden spoon until mixture begins to thicken and lose its gloss.

6. Add nuts and quickly turn out onto lightly greased surface and knead into a square approximately ¼ inch thick.

7. Cool until firm.

8. Cut into ¼-inch squares for dipping in Chocolate Coating.

Yield: Approximately 108 pieces.

Chapter 9
CARAMELS

The aristocrat of homemade candies might well be the caramel, a
smooth rich fudge-type sweet of tender, chewy consistency, hand-
dipped in a delicious Chocolate Coating. Although caramels are an
elegant member of the candy family, they are deceptively easy
to make.

I have gotten around the old time-consuming method for making
caramels, which takes at least two and one-half hours to evaporate
the water content in the milk or cream. This prolonged cooking also
has a tendency to cause the caramels to be tough and strong in
flavor. I use undiluted sweetened condensed milk, which has
already gone through the water-evaporation process. The result is a
superb caramel in approximately thirty minutes.

Caramels, if they are not to be coated with chocolate, must be cut
and wrapped after they are cool to prevent them from spreading.
Store them in an airtight container in a dry, cool place and they will
keep up to six months.

A few simple instructions, and you will be turning out the most
delicious caramels you ever tasted.

Caramel-Making Basics:

Step 1: You must stir the mixture often during cooking because of the rich butterfat content. Caramels have a tendency to scorch on the bottom of the pan.

Step 2: Do not use too much butter or oil when preparing the cooling pan, otherwise the finished caramel will be very greasy.

Step 3: Cut waxed paper or plastic wrap into sizes just large enough to fold over the top and across the ends of each caramel.

Basic Vanilla Caramels

(Recommended as Centers for Chocolate Coating)

Utensils:

1   2-quart heavy saucepan
1   wooden spoon
1   set measuring spoons
1   set measuring cups
Candy thermometer
1   pan, 9 x 9 x 2 inches
Waxed paper or plastic wrap

Ingredients:

1   cup (240 ml) butter
2¼ cups (540 ml) granulated sugar, sifted
¼   teaspoon (1.25 ml) salt
1   cup (240 ml) light corn syrup
1⅓ cups (320 ml) (one 14-ounce can)
    sweetened condensed milk
1   teaspoon (5 ml) vanilla
1   cup (240 ml) chopped nuts (optional)

Preparation:

1. Melt butter in saucepan over low heat.

2. Add sugar and salt and stir with wooden spoon until thoroughly blended.

3. Add corn syrup and, stirring constantly, gradually add the milk.

4. Start mixture boiling and clip on candy thermometer.

5. Cook over moderate heat, stirring as often as necessary to prevent scorching, until thermometer registers 248°F. or 120°C. (syrup forms a firm ball (p. 26) in cold water).

6. Remove from heat. Let stand for 5 minutes; add vanilla and nuts.

7. Quickly spread into lightly greased pan.

8. When cool, turn the block of candy out onto a smooth surface.

9. Cut into 1-inch squares with a large sharp knife.

10. Immediately wrap each caramel in waxed paper or plastic wrap.

Yield: 81 pieces.

Variations:

Chocolate Caramels: Add two 1-ounce squares (57 grams) of bitter chocolate, chopped, to mixture after butter is melted.

Butterscotch Caramels: Use 1 cup (240 ml) granulated sugar, sifted, and 1¼ cups (300 ml) light brown sugar, firmly packed.

Dipping Caramels:

Like fudge, caramels are firm and easily handled. Chocolate is the usual coating for caramels. Cut into ¾-inch squares and dip as soon as cool.

Chapter 10
TAFFY

This is a syrup of sugar or molasses cooked without stirring to just the right temperature. When it reaches the hard-ball or soft-crack stage, you let it cool and then pull it with your hands.

Taffy pulls were considered high-style frontier fun, and a positive test of brawn for groups of all ages. The old-fashioned taffy pull is here again! In fact it really never disappeared. It simply hid in the corner for a time; but with the trend toward stay-at-home parties, it's right back on the scene.

Why not have a party for all ages and enjoy the fun of a real taffy pull? A few instructions and you are ready.

Taffy-Making Basics:

Use a large heavy saucepan in order to give the molasses ample room to "boil up." In no other candy-making is there so much danger of "boiling over."

Step 1: Cook the taffy slowly during the last few minutes to prevent scorching. Molasses burns easily.

Step 2: When the syrup reaches the recommended temperature, pour it onto a lightly greased large baking sheet with sides. To keep from splattering yourself, pour very slowly and hold the pouring edge away from you just a few inches above the baking sheet. Place the baking sheet on a cooling rack to hasten the cooling process.

Step 3: Let the taffy cool to room temperature all by itself. Handling during the cooling period causes granulation. Add the flavoring at the end of the cooling period.

Step 4: Work the taffy with a spatula after the mass is cool enough to handle. When you test for coolness, you should not be able to feel any warmth from the underneath side of the baking sheet, and the mass should hold a finger imprint. With the candy spatula fold the taffy mass from outside to the center of the sheet. Continue this process until the candy is "worked" enough to gather in a ball. It is then ready to be pulled.

Step 5: Dip fingertips in cornstarch or rub them very lightly with butter to keep taffy from sticking to your fingers.

Step 6: Use only the thumb and fingers, rather than the whole hand, to pull taffy. This way there is less danger of having the candy stick to the hands.

Step 7: The time needed to pull a taffy depends on the temperature of the room, the speed at which you pull, and the humidity in the air. Taffy will not firm-up if pulled on a rainy day with high humidity.

Step 8: Notice the taffy's texture and color. When it is pulled enough, it shows small parallel ridges and becomes a light color. The candy must retain its shape and resist the scissors when cut.

Step 9: Shape pieces attractively by twisting the taffy into a rope. Cut one piece about an inch long, turn the rope half over, cut another piece about the same length, and continue to turn after each cutting. Keep the pieces separated after cutting.

Step 10: Use lightly buttered scissors for cutting taffy into pieces of the desired size. This is much faster than using a knife.

Step 11: Wrap each piece and store carefully in an airtight container at room temperature. If properly cooked and pulled, taffy will cream within a few hours. The taste of taffy leaves much to be desired until it has been stored overnight in a cool, dry place—cool but not cold. Do not refrigerate.

Taffy is most tender when consumed within a few days. It is not a particularly desirable candy for dipping in coating.

Basic Old-Fashioned Molasses Taffy

(Not Recommended as Centers for Coating)

During colonial times sugar was scarce, and taffy had to be made with sorghum syrup. This gave the candy a very strong taste. The recipe was modified and the flavor became gentler as sugar became more plentiful. Nowadays sorghum is available in nutrition centers.

Utensils:

1   3-quart heavy saucepan
1   wooden spoon
1   set measuring spoons
1   set measuring cups
Candy thermometer
1   spatula, 3 to 5 inches wide
1   large baking sheet with sides
Waxed paper or plastic wrap

Ingredients:

1   cup (240 ml) light molasses or sorghum
    syrup
¼   cup (60 ml) light corn syrup
1   cup (240 ml) granulated sugar, sifted
½   cup (120 ml) light brown sugar,
    firmly packed
¼   cup (60 ml) butter
1   tablespoon (15 ml) cider vinegar
⅛   teaspoon (.6 ml) baking soda

Preparation:

1. Lightly grease sides of saucepan.

2. Add molasses, corn syrup, sugars, butter, and vinegar. Cook over low heat, stirring constantly with the wooden spoon, until sugar is dissolved. You should not be able to feel sugar grains when you rub the spoon against the sides of the saucepan.

3. Remove from heat and, with a damp paper towel or small sponge, wipe any remaining grains from the sides of the pan above the liquid level.

4. Start the syrup boiling and clip on the candy thermometer.

5. Cook over low heat, stirring as necessary to keep mixture from scorching, until thermometer registers 265°F. or 129°C. (syrup forms a hard ball (p. 26) in cold water).

6. Remove from heat; thoroughly stir in baking soda.

7. Pour onto lightly greased baking sheet, holding the pouring edge of the saucepan away from you and only a few inches above the baking sheet.

8. Allow the syrup to cool to room temperature. Begin to work the taffy with the spatula after the mass is cool. Start by working outside edges to the center.

9. When cool enough to handle, gather into a ball.

10. Dip fingertips in cornstarch or rub them with butter and pull the taffy with thumb and fingers until light in color and texture.

11. Twist into a rope about ¾ inch in diameter and place on lightly greased surface.

12. Cut into 1-inch pieces with buttered scissors. Wrap each piece in waxed paper or plastic wrap.

Store in airtight container in cool, dry place—but do not refrigerate.

Yield: About 54 pieces.

Variation:

Humbugs: These are old-time Christmas treats. The fun name conjures demons, spirits, imposters, and gay packaging ideas to amuse a young shut-in.
    Cook syrup to 270°F. or 132°C. Add 6 drops of oil of peppermint to Basic Recipe as soon as syrup has cooled. Continue as in Basic Recipe. Give the taffy rope a single fat twist after each piece is cut—this will give each piece the traditional humbug shape.

Maple Taffy

(Not Recommended as Centers for Coating)

Long ago in sections of the country where maple trees were plentiful, candies made from maple sugar and syrup were inexpensive. Now even in those regions, the price of pure maple products is almost prohibitive. But it is fun to be extravagant occasionally and to make maple taffy with its special delicious flavor and subtle sweetness—not so sweet as candies made with all cane sugar.

Utensils:

1　2-quart heavy saucepan
1　wooden spoon
1　set measuring spoons
1　set measuring cups
Candy thermometer
1　spatula, 3 to 5 inches wide
1　large baking sheet with sides
Waxed paper or plastic wrap

Ingredients:

½　cup (120 ml) granulated sugar, sifted
¾　cup (180 ml) light corn syrup
¾　cup (180 ml) pure maple syrup
⅓　cup (80 ml) water
1½ tablespoons (22.5 ml) butter
⅛　teaspoon (.6 ml) baking soda

Preparation:

1. Lightly grease sides of saucepan.

2. Add sugar, syrups, and water. Cook over low heat, stirring constantly with the wooden spoon, until sugar is dissolved. You should not be able to feel sugar grains when you rub the spoon against the sides of the saucepan.

3. Remove from heat and, with a damp paper towel or small sponge, wipe any remaining grains from the sides of the pan above the liquid level.

4. Start the syrup boiling and clip on candy thermometer.

5. Cook over low heat, stirring as necessary to prevent mixture from scorching, until thermometer registers 275°F. or 135°C. (syrup forms a soft crack (p. 26) in cold water).

6. Remove from heat; thoroughly stir in butter and baking soda.

7. Pour onto lightly greased baking sheet, holding the pouring edge of the saucepan away from you and only a few inches above the baking sheet.

8. Allow the syrup to cool to room temperature. Begin to work the taffy with the spatula after the mass is cool. Start by turning outside edges to the center.

9. When cool enough to handle, gather into a ball.

10. Dip fingertips in cornstarch or rub them very lightly with butter and pull the taffy with thumb and fingers until light in color and texture.

11. Twist into a rope about ¾ inch in diameter and place on lightly greased surface.

12. Cut into 1-inch pieces, using buttered scissors. Wrap each piece in waxed paper or plastic wrap.

Store in airtight container in cool, dry place—but do not refrigerate.

Yield: About 36 pieces.

Salt-Water Taffy

(Not Recommended as Centers for Coating)

This is the famous candy sold along the Boardwalk at Atlantic City, where it is said to be made with sea water.

Utensils:

1 2-quart heavy saucepan
1 wooden spoon
1 set measuring spoons
1 set measuring cups
Candy thermometer
1 spatula, 3 to 5 inches wide
1 large baking sheet with sides
Waxed paper or plastic wrap

Ingredients:

1 cup (240 ml) water
2 cups (480 ml) granulated sugar, sifted
1 cup (240 ml) light corn syrup
1½ teaspoons (7.25 ml) salt, or use 1 teaspoon (5 ml) sea salt
2 teaspoons (10 ml) glycerine (obtain from pharmacy)
1 tablespoon (15 ml) butter
2 teaspoons (10 ml) vanilla

Preparation:

1. Lightly grease sides of saucepan.

2. Add water, sugar, corn syrup, salt, and glycerine. Cook over low heat, stirring constantly with the wooden spoon, until sugar is dissolved. You should not be able to feel sugar grains when you rub the spoon against the sides of the saucepan.

3. Remove from heat and, with a damp paper towel or small sponge, wipe any remaining grains from the sides of the pan above the liquid level.

4. Start the syrup boiling and clip on the candy thermometer.

5. Cook over medium-low heat, without stirring, until thermometer registers 262°F. or 128°C. (syrup forms a hard ball (p. 26) in cold water).

6. Remove from heat. Add butter and when butter is melted pour onto lightly greased baking sheet, holding the pouring edge of the saucepan away from you and only a few inches above the baking sheet.

7. Allow the syrup to cool to room temperature and add vanilla.

8. Begin to work the taffy with the spatula after the mass is cool. Start by turning outside edges to the center.

9. When cool enough to handle, gather in ball.

10. Dip fingertips in cornstarch or rub them very lightly with butter and pull the taffy with thumb and fingers until light in color and texture.

11. Twist into a rope about ¾ inch in diameter and place on lightly greased surface.

12. Cut into 1-inch pieces with buttered scissors. Wrap each piece in waxed paper or plastic wrap.

Store in airtight container in cool, dry place—but do not refrigerate.

Yield: About 54 pieces.

Variation:

Pastel Taffy: Use Coloring and Flavoring Charts (pp. 30-31) to create the pastel tints as sold along the Boardwalks. Remember that ¼ teaspoon (1.25 ml) flavoring oil equals 1 teaspoon (5 ml) flavoring extract.

Old-Fashioned Taffy Apples

Wicked witches, hats, and coal-black cats were part of the fun of all-night Halloween parties of our colonial ancestors. The harvest was over, permitting time for teen-age play.

These taffy apples are fine for immediate eating but do not keep well. After 48 hours the coating becomes very dry and brittle. I suggest these be made at parties where they will be consumed as part of the re-freshments.

To keep dipped apples from forming heavy bottoms tell the youngsters to plunge them into a bowl of ice water before placing them on a lightly greased baking sheet to harden.

Utensils:

1   2-quart heavy saucepan
1   wooden spoon
1   set measuring spoons
1   set measuring cups
Candy thermometer
Sticks for apples
Large baking sheet

Ingredients:

2   cups (480 ml) granulated sugar, sifted
¾   cup (180 ml) water
1   tablespoon (15 ml) light corn syrup
½   cup (120 ml) butter
1   teaspoon (5 ml) cider vinegar
½   cup (120 ml) light (coffee) cream
6-8 big red apples

Preparation:

1. Lightly grease sides of saucepan.

2. Add sugar, water, corn syrup, butter, vinegar, and cream. Cook over low heat, stirring constantly until sugar is dissolved. You should not be able to feel sugar grains when you rub the wooden spoon against the sides of the saucepan.

3. Remove from heat and, with a damp paper towel or small sponge, wipe any remaining grains from the sides of the pan above the liquid level.

4. Cook over low heat, stirring as necessary to prevent mixture from scorching, until thermometer registers 260°F. or 127°C. (syrup forms a hard ball (p. 26) in cold water).

5. Remove from heat.

6. Insert a stick into an apple and dip into syrup, then plunge into ice water and place on lightly greased baking sheet to harden. If the syrup becomes too firm for dipping, reheat slightly.

Variation:

Taffy Apples with Nut Coating: Dip the apples in the taffy syrup and then immediately roll them in finely chopped nuts—any kind.

Basic Pulled-Cream Candy

(Recommended as Centers for Chocolate Coating)

The recipe for this pulled candy came to me from my ancestors who carried it across the Ohio River in a wagon train lashed together with wild grapevines. A very special recipe indeed and tricky to make, it is the basis for pulled mints, candy canes, and creamy centers for chocolate dipping.

From a recipe that called for butter "the size of an egg" and other ingredients measured in the quaint culinary language of the day, it took my sister fourteen testings to perfect our favorite recipe for this book. The following are her cooking steps.

Pulled-Cream Candy-Making Basics:

Step 1: Make this candy on a day when the weather is very clear and the barometer steady.

Step 2: Do not substitute ingredients.

Step 3: The temperature at which the mixture is handled determines whether you have a granulated mess or smooth creamy candy beyond compare. This mixture should be cooled as rapidly as possible to room temperature which should still be cool. My best results came from placing a lightly buttered baking sheet over a cooling rack and then pouring the hot syrup onto the sheet. Do not pour the syrup onto the baking sheet and then attempt to transfer it to the cooling rack. This additional movement will cause immediate crystallization of the syrup. The cooling rack allows for circulation of air, which speeds the cooling period. Cool the mixture until the bottom of the baking sheet actually feels cold when you place the palm of your hand against it.

Step 4: Begin to handle candy as for pulling taffy. Divide the cooked candy into three portions and pull each separately. This is much easier than trying to pull the entire mass. If insufficiently pulled, this candy will not "cream." It must have a rather tough resistant feel and be pure white, which will indicate it has been pulled sufficiently.

Step 5: The old recipe reads, "The candy will be chewy at first but begins to 'cream' within a few hours." Store in airtight container between layers of waxed paper in cool, dry place—but do not refrigerate.

Utensils:

1   3-quart heavy saucepan
1   wooden spoon
1   set measuring spoons
1   set measuring cups
Candy thermometer
Electric mixer (optional)
Large mixing bowl
1   spatula, 3 to 5 inches wide
1   large baking sheet with sides

Ingredients:

1   cup (240 ml) water
3   cups (720 ml) granulated sugar, sifted
1½ tablespoons (22.5 ml) heavy (whipping) cream
1½ teaspoons (7.5 ml) white vinegar
½   teaspoon (2.5 ml) salt
2   tablespoons (30 ml) butter
4-5 drops oil of peppermint or other flavoring
Food coloring (optional)

Preparation:

1. Lightly grease sides of saucepan and add water.

2. Combine the sugar, cream, vinegar, salt, and butter in mixing bowl. Cream as if making a cake, using electric mixer or wooden spoon.

3. Bring water to full boil and remove from heat; gradually stir the creamed mixture into the hot water with a wooden spoon.

4. Cook over low heat, stirring constantly with the wooden spoon, until sugar is dissolved. You should not be able to feel sugar grains when you rub the spoon against the sides of the saucepan.

5. Remove from heat and, with a damp paper towel or small sponge, wipe any remaining grains from the sides of the pan above the liquid level.

6. Return the mixture to moderate heat. Cover the pan long enough for the mixture to boil, which should take 2 or 3 minutes—no more!

7. Uncover the pan and wipe the sides *again* to remove any stray sugar grains. This step is a *must.*

8. Start the syrup boiling again and clip on the candy thermometer.

9. Cook over medium-low heat, without stirring until thermometer registers 258°F. or 126°C. (syrup forms a hard ball (p. 26) in cold water).

10. Remove from heat and pour mixture in a slow, steady stream onto a lightly buttered baking sheet placed over a cooling rack. Cool until the mixture is at room temperature.

11. Add flavoring and begin to work the candy with the spatula. Start by turning outside edges to the center with spatula.

12. As it thickens, gather the mass into a ball for easier handling.

13. Dip fingertips in cornstarch or rub them lightly with butter and pull the candy with thumb and fingers until it is white and ridges form.

14. Twist into a rope about ¾ inch in diameter and place on lightly buttered surface.

15. Cut into 1-inch pieces, using buttered scissors.

To store, wrap each piece in waxed paper or plastic wrap or place pieces between layers of waxed paper in airtight container in cool, dry place—but do not refrigerate.

Yield: About 80 pieces.

Variations:

Candy Canes: Before you begin the pulling, divide the mixture into two portions. Leave one portion white and tint the second with red food color or coloring paste. After each portion is pulled into a rope ½ inch in diameter, twist the two together to form one rope and place on lightly greased surface. Cut into 4- to 5-inch lengths, using buttered scissors. Curl one end over to form cane.

Old-Fashioned Buttercrème Mints: Prepare as for Candy Canes (above). Cut into 1-inch pieces, using buttered scissors. Wrap each piece in waxed paper or plastic wrap. Store in airtight container in cool, dry place—but do not refrigerate.

Yield: 80 mints.

Buttercrème Centers for Dipping in Chocolate Coating: Everyone agrees that these are the most delicious centers they have ever eaten. Prepare Basic Recipe (p. 105). Before pulling is begun, divide the mixture into as many portions as the number of flavors desired. See Coloring and Flavoring Charts (pp. 30-31). Pull candy (as in Basic Recipe) into a rope about ½ inch in diameter. Cut into ½-inch pieces, using buttered scissors. Form each piece into a small ball and place on lightly greased surface. Store in airtight container and let "cream" overnight in cool, dry place—but do not refrigerate. Remove the centers from the container to glaze over the surface before dipping in chocolate.

Chapter 11
BRITTLE

This is the oldest and simplest form of candy-making. A brittle is just what the name implies. For instance, can't you almost taste the rich crispness of a crunchy brittle? If you develop a sudden and urgent sweet tooth, it takes only a few minutes to stir up a batch.

The following is a selection of recipes, both regional and international, nutritious, and tasty. Simple for adults and teen-agers to make, this candy has only a few musts to remember.

Brittle-Making Basics:

Step 1: You must use a heavy saucepan for cooking the syrup because the concentrated mixture has a tendency to scorch.

Step 2: Wipe sugar grains from the sides of the saucepan as directed in each recipe so there will be no chance of crystallizing the syrup before it cooks to the proper temperature.

Step 3: Warm nuts unless otherwise stated in recipe because, if they are cold, they will cool the syrup too much for spreading on a baking sheet.

Step 4: Add baking soda to make a delicate, refined, and porous brittle.

Step 5: Pour the brittle—to a depth of ⅛ to ¼ inch—onto a large oiled baking sheet with sides. Never pour it into a small pan with sides, as it cannot then be stretched to a thin sheet.

Step 6: Stretch a brittle by these steps:
a. Pour it as quickly as possible onto the oiled baking sheet.
b. Press it out with a spatula and, as soon as it can be touched, lift the edges and pull gently. At this point you may don clean white cotton gloves to stretch the warm mass out until it becomes very thin.

Step 7: When the brittle is cool and firm break into irregular eating-size pieces with a small mallet.

Step 8: Although most brittles can be eaten while they are buttery warm, they are better if stored in airtight containers and aged for 24 hours.

Shoe Box Peanut Brittle

(Not Recommended as Centers for Coating)
This is the real old-fashioned peanut brittle, sold in bulk at the country general store. It acquired its name from the fact that the recipe just about filled a small-size shoe box for mailing.
   The following recipe has been in my family for many generations. It is dedicated to the memory of my father—his very most favorite candy.

Utensils:

1   3-quart heavy saucepan
1   wooden spoon
1   set measuring spoons
1   set measuring cups
Candy thermometer
1   spatula, 3 to 5 inches wide
1   large baking sheet with sides

Ingredients:

2   cups (480 ml) salted peanuts
1½ cups (360 ml) granulated sugar, sifted
1½ cups (360 ml) light corn syrup
¼   cup (60 ml) water
2   tablespoons (30 ml) butter

Combine the following:

1   teaspoon (5 ml) baking soda
½   teaspoon (2.5 ml) vanilla
2   teaspoons (10 ml) cold water

Preparation:

1. Place peanuts in shallow pan. Bake at 275°F. or 135°C. until heated through. Do not roast.

2. Lightly grease sides of saucepan.

3. Add sugar, corn syrup, and ¼ cup (60 ml) water. Cook over low heat, stirring constantly with the wooden spoon, until sugar is dissolved. You should not be able to feel sugar grains when you rub the spoon against the sides of the pan.

4. Remove from heat and, with a damp paper towel or small sponge, wipe any grains from the sides of the pan above the liquid level.

5. Start the syrup boiling and clip on the candy thermometer.

6. Cook over low heat, without stirring, until thermometer registers 275°F. or 135°C. (syrup forms a soft crack (p. 26) in cold water).

7. Remove thermometer; lower heat.

8. Add butter and peanuts; cook, stirring constantly, for 5 minutes.

9. Clip candy thermometer back on the side of the pan; cook, stirring constantly, to 300°F. or 149°C. (syrup forms hard crack (p. 26) in cold water).

10. Remove from heat; stir in the soda, vanilla, and cold water mixture and continue to stir for 30 seconds. Candy will foam.

11. Pour onto well-oiled baking sheet. Cool until surface is barely warm to the fingers. Then, with a spatula turn the mass over and with your hands pull and stretch as thin as possible.

12. Break into irregular eating-size pieces and cool.
Store in airtight container in layers separated by sheets of waxed paper.

Yield: Approximately 1½ pounds (682 grams).

Sandra's "Noent" (Honey-Nut Brittle)

(Not Recommended as Centers for Coating)

Chanukah is a time of joy and festivities for the Jewish people. I am indebted to Libby Hillman, cooking teacher, author, and friend, for sharing this recipe for a traditional sweet served during the eight days of celebrating.

Utensils:

1   6-quart heavy saucepan
1   wooden spoon
1   tablespoon (15 ml) measure
1   cup (240 ml) measure
Candy thermometer
1   spatula, 3 to 5 inches wide
1   large marble slab or 2 large baking sheets

Ingredients:

3   pounds (1363 grams) dark honey
6   tablespoons (90 ml) fresh lemon juice
7   cups (1680 ml) nuts, chopped

Preparation:

1. Lightly grease sides of saucepan.

2. Add honey and lemon juice. Cook over low heat, stirring constantly until well blended.

3. Add nuts and continue stirring for about 20 minutes or until the mixture is dark in color and very thick. It should register 245°F. or 118°C. on thermometer.

4. Lightly oil marble or baking sheets and wet down with ice water; turn candy onto wet surface.

5. With a spatula spread mixture to ½-inch thickness. Keep marble and mixture wet with ice water until candy hardens.

6. Cut into eating-size pieces (squares or diamonds) and remove to a flat dry surface.

This candy can be refrigerated or frozen.

Note: Libby says, "Some people add a bit of ground ginger to taste to the honey and lemon juice."

Yield: Approximately 4 pounds (1818 grams).

Irish Butterscotch

(Not Recommended as Centers for Coating)
This brittle may be finely crushed, mixed
with dipping chocolate, and dropped from a
teaspoon onto waxed paper.

Utensils:

1   2-quart heavy saucepan
1   wooden spoon
1   set measuring spoons
1   set measuring cups
Candy thermometer
1   spatula, 3 to 5 inches wide
1   large baking sheet with sides

Ingredients:

1   cup (240 ml) granulated sugar, sifted
½   cup (120 ml) light brown sugar,
      firmly packed
1   teaspoon (5 ml) cider vinegar
½   cup (120 ml) light corn syrup
¼   cup (60 ml) water
½   cup (120 ml) butter, cut in small pieces
½   teaspoon (2.5 ml) vanilla

Preparation:

1. Lightly grease sides of saucepan.

2. Add sugars, vinegar, corn syrup, and water.
Cook over low heat, stirring constantly with
the wooden spoon, until sugar is dissolved.
You should not be able to feel sugar grains
when you rub the spoon against the sides of
the saucepan.

3. Remove from heat and, with a damp paper
towel or small sponge, wipe any remaining
grains from the sides of the pan above the
liquid level.

4. Start the syrup boiling and clip on the
candy thermometer.

5. Cook over low heat, adding butter bit by
bit while stirring constantly, until thermometer registers 300°F. or 149°C. (syrup
forms a hard crack (p. 26) in cold water).

6. Remove from heat; stir in vanilla.

7. Pour onto well-oiled baking sheet. Cool
until surface is just barely warm to the
fingers. Then, with a spatula, turn the mass
over and with your hands pull and stretch as
thin as possible.

8. Break into irregular eating-size pieces and
cool.

Store in airtight containers in layers separated by sheets of waxed paper.

Yield: About 1 pound (454 grams).

Kentucky Lemon Brittle

(Not Recommended as Centers for Coating)
My twenty-year-old niece, Cathy, has taken up our family hobby of seaching for unpublished candy recipes. She received the following prize from a grandmotherly friend, Cora Cannon. Cathy thinks readers should know this candy does not have the burnt-sugar taste of regular peanut brittle and comes out with a pretty yellow tint. She tested the recipe and used pulverized popcorn salt to coat the peanuts. In her words, "It sticks to the peanuts."

Utensils:

1   2-quart heavy saucepan
1   wooden spoon
1   set measuring spoons
1   set measuring cups
Candy thermometer
1   spatula, 3 to 5 inches wide
1   large baking sheet with sides

Ingredients:

1½ cups (360 ml) unroasted peanuts
¼   teaspoon (1.25 ml) pulverized popcorn
      salt
½   cup (120 ml) light corn syrup
1½ cups (360 ml) water
1   cup (240 ml) granulated sugar, sifted
1½ teaspoons (7.5 ml) butter (do not
      substitute)
½   teaspoon (2.5 ml) lemon extract, or use
      ¼ teaspoon (1.25 ml) oil of lemon for
      stronger flavor

Preparation:

1. Mix the peanuts with the popcorn salt and set aside.

2. Lightly grease sides of saucepan.

3. Add corn syrup, water, and sugar. Cook over low heat, stirring constantly with the wooden spoon, until sugar is dissolved. You should not be able to feel sugar grains when you rub the spoon against the sides of the saucepan.

4. Remove from heat and, with a damp paper towel or small sponge, wipe any remaining grains from the sides of the pan above the liquid level.

5. Start the syrup boiling and clip on the candy thermometer.

6. Cook over low heat, without stirring, until thermometer registers 295°F. or 146°C. (syrup forms a hard crack (p. 26) in cold water).

7. Remove from heat; gently stir in butter, peanuts, and—last—the flavoring.

8. Pour onto well-oiled baking sheet. Cool until surface is just barely warm to the fingers. Then, with a spatula turn the mass over and with your hands pull and stretch as thin as possible.

9. Break into irregular eating-size pieces and cool.

Store in airtight container in layers separated by sheets of waxed paper.

Yield: About 1 pound (454 grams).

Sesame Seed Brittle

(Not Recommended as Centers for Coating)

The recipe directly below is from Georgia. Sesame seeds came to Savannah during the days of slave trading with Africans who called them "benne," a name still used in the South and Africa.

Most specialty-food stores carry tins of this crunchy candy. Prepare your own for gift giving.

Utensils:

1 shallow pan
1 2-quart heavy saucepan
1 wooden spoon
1 set measuring spoons
1 set measuring cups
Candy thermometer
1 spatula, 3 to 5 inches wide
1 large baking sheet with sides

Ingredients:

1 cup (240 ml) sesame seeds
1½ cups (360 ml) granulated sugar, sifted
½ cup (120 ml) honey
2 tablespoons (30 ml) water
1 teaspoon (5 ml) fresh lemon juice
¼ teaspoon (1.25 ml) ground cinnamon

Preparation:

1. Place sesame seeds in shallow pan. Bake at 275°F. or 135°C. until lightly roasted. Stir frequently to prevent burning.

2. Set aside.

3. Lightly grease sides of saucepan.

4. Add sugar, honey, water, and lemon juice. Cook over low heat, stirring constantly with the wooden spoon, until sugar is dissolved.

You should not be able to feel sugar grains when you rub the spoon against the sides of the saucepan.

5. Remove from heat and, with a damp paper towel or small sponge, wipe any remaining grains from the sides of the pan above the liquid level.

6. Start the syrup boiling and clip on the candy thermometer.

7. Cook over low heat, without stirring, until thermometer registers 300°F. or 149°C. (syrup forms a hard crack (p. 26) in cold water).

8. Remove from heat; gently stir in cinnamon and sesame seeds.

9. Pour onto well-oiled baking sheet. Cool until surface is barely warm to the fingers.

10. Mark in 1-inch squares and break pieces apart.

Store in airtight container in layers separated by sheets of waxed paper.

Yield: About 1 pound (454 grams).

Variation:

Honey-Almond Brittle: Omit cinnamon and sesame seeds. Substitute 1 cup (240 ml) slivered roasted almonds. Stir in 1½ tablespoons (22.5 ml) butter while adding almonds.

Honeycomb Brittle

(Recommended for Chocolate Coating)

Honeycomb Brittle is the basis for chocolate-coated chips. During the cooking process the candy will foam when the soda is added, so be certain to use the recommended large-size cooking pan. The honeycomb effect from which the candy derives its name comes from the foaming; a chemical reaction makes the layers separate.

Utensils:

1   3-quart heavy saucepan
1   wooden spoon
1   set measuring spoons
1   set measuring cups
Candy thermometer
1   pan, 9 x 12 x 2 inches

Ingredients:

¾   cup (180 ml) water
2   cups (480 ml) granulated sugar, sifted
2   tablespoons (30 ml) liquid honey
2   tablespoons (30 ml) cider vinegar
2   tablespoons (30 ml) butter
1   teaspoon (5 ml) baking soda dissolved in
    4 teaspoons (20 ml) hot water

Preparation:

1. Lightly grease sides of saucepan.

2. Add water, sugar, honey, vinegar, and butter. Cook over low heat, stirring constantly with the wooden spoon, until sugar is dissolved. You should not be able to feel sugar grains when you rub the spoon against the sides of the saucepan.

3. Remove from heat and, with a damp paper towel or small sponge, wipe any remaining grains from the sides of the pan above the liquid level.

4. Start the syrup boiling and clip on the candy thermometer.

5. Cook slowly, without stirring, until thermometer registers 300°F. or 149°C. (syrup forms a hard crack (p. 26) in cold water).

6. Remove from heat and stir in dissolved soda mixture.

7. Pour into well-oiled pan. Cool until surface is just barely warm to the fingers.

8. Cut into rectangles about ½ inch wide and 1 inch long.

9. Cool to room temperature for dipping.

Yield: 216 thin pieces.

Chapter 12
TOFFEE AND CRUNCH

The preparation of toffee and crunch is so easy they are great candies for the novice candy cook to try.

Considered the rich cousins of the simpler brittles, toffee is usually dressed up with a chocolate coating and crunch is made with extra-lavish quantities of butter.

Toffee and Crunch-Making Basics:

Step 1: The butter content is high in both toffee and crunch, so there is no danger of crystallizing the finished products by over-stirring during the cooking process. But be sure to use real butter. Any substitute shortening will cause the ingredients to separate during the cooking.

Step 2: Nuts can be added to the cooked syrup just before it is poured into the pan. Sliver or chop large nuts like almonds and Brazil nuts. Leave smaller nuts whole, or use the pieces and bits left over from baking and other candy-making. If the nuts are to be placed in the pan first, and the cooked syrup then poured over them, the nuts must be very lightly roasted. See p. 28 for the method.

Step 3: Toffee and crunch are both poured into a pan to harden and then either cut or broken into pieces with a mallet. You may pour the mixture onto a buttered baking sheet with sides and then form it into a square, but I find pouring into a lightly greased pan easier.

Step 4: Both toffee and crunch are good keepers because of the high butter content. They can stay refrigerated or frozen almost indefinitely. In all cases store the candies in airtight containers in layers separated by sheets of waxed paper.

Peanut Butter Toffee

(Recommended as Centers for Chocolate Coating)
In our family we encourage teen-age cooks by giving them free rein in the kitchen. The juniors judged this recipe "Excellent, easy to make, and foolproof. Rich, Rich, Rich!" Cut into small squares and dipped in Chocolate Coating, it has become a family favorite.

Utensils:

1   1-quart double boiler
1   2-quart heavy saucepan
1   wooden spoon
1   set measuring spoons
1   set measuring cups
Candy thermometer
1   spatula, 3 to 5 inches wide
1   pan, 8 x 8 x 2 inches

Ingredients:

1   cup (240 ml) peanut butter, creamy or chunky
1   cup (240 ml) granulated sugar, sifted
1/3 cup (80 ml) light corn syrup
1/3 cup (80 ml) water

Preparation:

1. Heat the peanut butter in top of double boiler over simmering water and keep warm until candy syrup is cooked.

2. Lightly grease sides of saucepan.

3. Add sugar, corn syrup, and water. Cook over low heat, stirring constantly with the wooden spoon, until sugar is dissolved. You should not be able to feel sugar grains when you rub the spoon against the sides of the saucepan.

4. Remove from heat and, with a damp paper towel or small sponge, wipe any remaining grains from the sides of the pan above the liquid level.

5. Start the syrup boiling and clip on the candy thermometer.

6. Cook over low heat, without stirring, until thermometer registers 310°F. or 154°C. (syrup forms a hard crack (p. 26) in cold water).

7. Remove from heat; add warm peanut butter and stir until thoroughly blended.

8. Immediately pour into lightly greased pan.

9. With spatula spread to an even depth of ½ inch.

10. With a knife make deep indents to mark 1-inch squares.

11. When cold turn out onto smooth surface and break pieces apart.

Yield: 64 squares.

Butter Almond Toffee

(Recommended as Centers for Chocolate Coating)
This is a very old recipe, which is also known as English toffee.

Utensils:

1   2-quart heavy saucepan
1   wooden spoon
1   set measuring spoons
1   set measuring cups
Candy thermometer
1   spatula, 3 to 5 inches wide
1   pan, 9 x 9 x 2 inches

Ingredients:

1   cup (240 ml) almonds, lightly roasted and chopped or slivered
1   cup (240 ml) butter
1   cup (240 ml) granulated sugar, sifted

⅓   cup (80 ml) light brown sugar, firmly packed
2   tablespoons (30 ml) cold water
½   teaspoon (2.5 ml) baking soda
1   cup (240 ml) semisweet chocolate bits or melted dipping chocolate

Preparation:

1. Sprinkle ½ cup (120 ml) of the almonds evenly on bottom of lightly buttered 9 x 9 x 2 inch pan.

2. Melt the butter in saucepan over low heat.

3. Add sugar and water. Cook over low heat, stirring constantly with the wooden spoon, until sugar is dissolved and mixture comes to a boil.

4. Clip on candy thermometer and continue to cook over low heat, stirring constantly. To prevent separation of butter and sugar keep mixture boiling until thermometer registers 280°F. or 138°C. (syrup forms a soft crack (p. 26) in cold water).

5. Remove from heat; quickly stir in the soda and blend thoroughly.

6. Turn at once into prepared almond-lined pan.

7. Let cool for 5 minutes. Then quickly sprinkle chocolate bits over candy. (Heat will melt the chocolate.)

8. With the spatula spread the melting chocolate evenly over the toffee.

9. Sprinkle the remaining almonds over the chocolate and press down lightly with the spatula.

10. With a knife make deep indents to mark 1-inch squares. When cool, turn out onto smooth surface and break pieces apart.

Yield: 81 squares.

Butter Crunch

(Recommended as Centers for Chocolate Coating)

An old-fashioned heavy iron skillet is the best possible cooking utensil for making butter crunch. Iron keeps heat constant throughout the cooking process, thus effectively preventing the sugar and butter from separating. Lacking an iron skillet, use the heaviest type of cooking pan available.

Utensils:

1   9- to 10-inch heavy iron skillet
1   wooden spoon
1   cup (240 ml) measure
Candy thermometer
1   spatula, 3 to 5 inches wide
1   pan, 8 x 8 x 2 inches

Ingredients:

1   cup (240 ml) butter
1   cup (240 ml) granulated sugar, sifted
1   cup (240 ml) nutmeats, finely ground but
    not roasted
1   cup (240 ml) semisweet chocolate bits or
    melted dipping chocolate
1   cup (240 ml) lightly roasted nutmeats,
    finely ground (optional)

Preparation:

1. Melt the butter in skillet over low heat. Slowly add sugar.

2. Cook over low heat, stirring constantly with the wooden spoon, until sugar is dissolved and mixture comes to a boil.

3. Clip on candy thermometer. Cook over low heat, stirring constantly. To prevent separation of butter and sugar keep mixture

boiling until thermometer registers 300°F. or 149°C. (syrup forms a hard crack (p. 26) in cold water).

4. Remove from heat and quickly stir in the unroasted nuts.

5. Turn at once into lightly greased pan.

6. Let cool for 5 minutes. Then quickly sprinkle chocolate bits over candy. (Heat will melt the chocolate.)

7. With the spatula spread the chocolate evenly over the crunch.

8. If you are using the roasted nuts, sprinkle them over the chocolate and press down lightly with the spatula.

9. When cool, turn out onto smooth surface and break into eating-size pieces with a mallet.

Yield: About 1⅓ pounds (605 grams).

Chapter 13
FONDANT

Fondant is a thick, creamy sugar paste that turns into the basis of mint patties, coated creams, and many other different melt-in-your mouth candies. It is made from four simple ingredients: sugar, water, flavoring, and corn syrup to help dissolve the sugar so the candy will be smooth. The ingredients are cooked, cooled, kneaded, and then stored in an airtight container to ripen the flavor and texture.

As a child I was slightly prejudiced against fondant. I knew it as a bland homemade candy lightly flavored with vanilla, rolled into little balls, and sandwiched between two nut halves. I have learned from my own candy-making that cooks are to blame when fondant is unappealing. Fondant flavors can include almond, orange, lemon, cherry, chocolate, peppermint or wintergreen, coffee, or maple, as well as the classic vanilla. Fondant can be tinted any color of the rainbow and shaped. After you have reviewed the technique of producing a nice creamy, flavorful fondant, have fun expressing your creative talents by molding the confection into clever shapes.

Fondant-Making Basics:

The primary object in fondant-making is to produce a creamy mass in which the sugar grains are of the smallest possible size. Follow these steps carefully:

Step 1: Choose the proper weather! Dry, cool weather, with the barometric pressure normal and steady, is essential. In any other weather, make a fondant from the *Quick and Easy* section (pp. 41-46).

Step 2: Measure and place the water and sugar in a heavy saucepan.

Step 3: Place over low heat and stir constantly until sugar is dissolved. Do *not* let mixture come to a boil.

Step 4: Remove from heat. Add any other ingredients the recipe calls for.

Step 5: Using a damp paper towel or small sponge, wipe any remaining sugar grains from the sides of the pan above the water level.

Step 6: Return the dissolved water-sugar mixture to moderate heat.

Step 7: Cover the pan long enough for the mixture to boil, which should take 2 or 3 minutes—no more! During the boiling process the steam washes sugar grains from the sides of the pan, but when you uncover it again you *must* wipe the sides of the pan *again* to remove any newly formed grains. Remember one stray grain can multiply and make the entire mixture grainy.

Step 8: Clip on the candy thermometer. Cook at a slow boil, without stirring, until the thermometer registers the temperature recommended in the recipe.

Step 9: Pour mixture in a slow, steady stream onto a slightly dampened baking sheet or large platter. Do *not* scrape pan. Cool to lukewarm (110°F. or 43°C.).

Step 10: Work fondant with a wide spatula or wooden spoon by lifting and folding edges toward the center. When the candy loses its translucency and begins to become opaque and creamy, gather into a ball and knead lightly with buttered hands. Continue kneading until mass is smooth and creamy. Even experienced cooks sometimes cook fondant until it is too hard to knead into the desired creamy mass. If this has happened to you, wrap the fondant in a steaming hot Turkish towel which you have wrung out. Then cover the wrapped ball with a large mixing bowl. Let stand for about 15 minutes.

Step 11: Wrap fondant in waxed paper and store in airtight container to ripen for at least several hours (2 to 4 days is better). Most fondants can be stored in the refrigerator for 10 days, provided the container is airtight, or they can be kept in the freezer up to 2 months.

Step 12: If fondant is too soft to form good centers, either from over-kneading or lengthy storage, knead into it a small amount of confectioners' sugar. This will make the fondant firmer. However, added at this stage, the sugar will also make it slightly coarse and less creamy.

Basic White Fondant

(Recommended as Centers for Chocolate, Summer, or Fondant Coating)

Utensils:

1   3-quart heavy saucepan
1   wooden spoon
1   set measuring cups
Candy thermometer
1   spatula, 3 to 5 inches wide
1   large baking sheet with sides

Ingredients:

1⅓ cups (320 ml) water
3   cups (720 ml) granulated sugar, sifted
¼   teaspoon (1.25 ml) salt
⅓   cup (80 ml) light corn syrup
1   teaspoon (5 ml) vanilla

Preparation:

1. Lightly grease sides of saucepan.

2. Add water, sugar, salt, and corn syrup. Cook over low heat, stirring constantly with the wooden spoon until sugar is dissolved. You should not be able to feel sugar grains when you rub the spoon against the sides of the saucepan.

3. Remove from heat and, with a damp paper towel or small sponge, wipe any remaining grains from the sides of the pan above the liquid level.

4. Return the mixture to moderate heat. Cover the pan long enough for the mixture to boil, which should take 2 or 3 minutes—no more!

5. Uncover the pan and again wipe the sides to remove any stray sugar grains. This step is a *must.*

6. Start the syrup boiling again and clip on the candy thermometer.

7. Cook over low heat, without stirring, until thermometer registers 239°F. or 115°C. (syrup forms a soft ball (p. 26) in cold water).

8. Remove from heat and pour mixture in a slow, steady stream onto a damp baking sheet. Do *not* scrape pan.

9. Cool to lukewarm. The bottom of the baking sheet should feel just warm, not hot.

10. Add vanilla and work fondant with spatula by lifting and folding edges of candy mass toward the center.

11. When the candy loses its translucency and begins to become opaque, gather into a ball and knead with buttered hands only until the mass is smooth and creamy and the ball holds together. Otherwise it may become too soft.

12. Wrap fondant ball in waxed paper and store in airtight container in refrigerator to ripen—for at least several hours.

Yield: About 108 small centers.

Variations:

Chocolate Fondant: Omit vanilla and add 5 tablespoons (75 ml) Dutch cocoa to water, sugar, salt, and corn syrup mixture.

Coffee Fondant: Omit water and substitute 1⅓ cups (320 ml) strong coffee.

Lemon and Orange Fondant: Omit vanilla and substitute 1 teaspoon (5 ml) dried lemon peel or 1 tablespoon (15 ml) dried orange peel. Do not use freshly grated lemon or orange peel because the acidity of the fresh peel is very likely to cause the fondant to liquefy before it can be shaped for dipping. Oil of lemon or orange may be substituted for the dried peel. See Coloring and Flavoring Charts (pp. 30-31).

Cherry Fondant: Omit vanilla and substitute ½ teaspoon (2.5 ml) cherry extract and 1 cup (240 ml) chopped candied cherries.

Peppermint Creams: Omit vanilla and substitute 8-10 drops of oil of peppermint, or use 1 teaspoon (5 ml) peppermint extract. A larger amount will dilute the fondant too much for molding. Mold into circles no larger than a quarter and approximately ½ inch thick. Crisscross with tines of fork before setting aside to glaze for dipping.

Coconut Fondant: Add 1½ cups (360 ml) dried coconut just before forming mass into ball.

Pineapple Fondant: Omit vanilla and substitute 1 teaspoon (5 ml) pineapple extract. Tint pale yellow.

Raspberry Fondant: Omit vanilla and substitute 1 teaspoon (5 ml) raspberry extract. Tint with at least 8 drops of red food coloring and 1 drop of blue for desired shade.

Rum-Raisin Fondant: Omit vanilla and add 1 teaspoon (5 ml) rum extract and ½ cup (120 ml) finely chopped dark raisins.

Brown Sugar Fondant: Use 1½ cups (360 ml) granulated sugar, sifted, and 1½ cups (360 ml) firmly packed brown sugar in place of 3 cups (720 ml) granulated sugar.

Buttercrème Fondant: Omit water and substitute whole milk. Add 1 tablespoon (15 ml) butter to mixture after it has been poured onto baking sheet.

Cherry or Nut Fondant Balls: Form ripened fondant into ½-inch balls. Press between two halves of candied cherries or nutmeats.

Stuffed Dried Fruit: Cut dates and prunes in half lengthwise; remove the pits and stuff with small amounts of fondant.

Fondant Loaves: Mix ½ cup (120 ml) chopped dried fruit and ½ cup (120 ml) chopped nutmeats into ripened fondant. Pack into small loaf pan lined with lightly greased foil. Let stand until firm. Unmold onto smooth surface. Cut into thin slices.

Tutti-Fruitti Fondant: Omit vanilla and substitute 1 teaspoon (5 ml) almond extract. Mix into ripened fondant 1 cup (240 ml) of chopped mixture of raisins, dates, figs, candied cherries, citron, orange peel, or other candied fruit. Use a combination of at least three of the above. Form into one large ball. Flatten slightly to shape in the traditional holiday flat cakes. Let cake stand for 1 hour and cut into thin wedges. Perfect for gift giving if wrapped in clear plastic and tied with a gay ribbon and sprig of holly.

Dipping Fondant Centers:

The softest, creamiest of all candy centers are made from cooked fondants. Softness is of great importance. The centers become softer after coating, but if they stand around and get too dry before being coated, they will never have the desired creaminess.

To make centers for dipping in Chocolate, Summer, or Fondant Coating, shape ripened fondant into a long roll about ½ inch in diameter. Cut the roll into pieces ½ inch long. Then roll each piece lightly between palms of hands into balls or ovals, whichever shape you desire. If creams tend to be sticky, use a small amount of cornstarch on hands. Do not make pieces too large. They will look much larger after they are dipped, and except for Easter-egg centers and other special holiday forms, candies should be petite.

I like to make centers and freeze them in quantity so that when I dip them in coating I will have a variety of flavors. If you freeze them, be sure to defrost them in their airtight container well ahead of time. They must be at room-temperature to achieve the desired final glazed-over look. Centers that are cold will develop gray streaks after being dipped.

Maple Cream Fondant

(Recommended as Centers for Chocolate or Summer Coating)

Repeated testings of this fondant proved it to be the most reliable recipe for the novice attempting her first fondant-dipping venture. Easy to make and with a delicate taste treat compared to maple creams made with artificial flavoring and coloring. Because it is softer than Basic White Fondant it must be cooked to a slightly higher temperature of 240° F. or 116° C. The recipe produces a perfect center for those delicious chocolate-covered maple creams.

Utensils:

1   2-quart heavy saucepan
1   wooden spoon
1   set measuring spoons
1   set measuring cups
Candy thermometer
1   spatula, 3 to 5 inches wide
1   large baking sheet with sides

Ingredients:

¾   cup (180 ml) water
2   cups (480 ml) granulated sugar, sifted
⅔   cup (160 ml) pure maple syrup
1   teaspoon (5 ml) vanilla

Preparation:

1. Lightly grease sides of saucepan.

2. Add water, sugar, and maple syrup. Cook over low heat, stirring constantly with the wooden spoon, until sugar is dissolved. You should not be able to feel sugar grains when you rub the spoon against the sides of the saucepan.

3. Remove from heat and, with a damp paper towel or small sponge, wipe any remaining grains from the sides of the pan above the liquid level.

4. Return the mixture to moderate heat. Cover the pan long enough for the mixture to boil, which should take 2 or 3 minutes—no more!

5. Uncover the pan and again wipe the sides to remove any stray sugar grains. This step is a *must.*

6. Start the syrup boiling again and clip on the candy thermometer.

7. Cook over low heat, without stirring, until thermometer registers 240°F. or 116°C. (syrup forms a soft ball (p. 26) in cold water).

8. Remove from heat and pour mixture in a slow, steady stream onto a damp baking sheet. Do *not* scrape pan.

9. Cool to lukewarm. The bottom of the baking sheet should feel just warm, not hot.

10. Add vanilla and work fondant with spatula by lifting and folding edges of candy mass toward the center.

11. When the candy loses its translucency and begins to become opaque, gather into a ball and knead with buttered hands only until the mass is smooth and creamy and the ball holds together. Otherwise it may become too soft and creamy.

12. Wrap fondant ball in waxed paper and store in airtight container in refrigerator to ripen—for at least several hours.

Yield: About 80 small oval centers.

Easy-Do Chocolate-Covered Cherries

The following is from the recipe files of Alice Young, Chairman of the Home Economics Department of the Martinsville, Virginia, school system. These candies are recommended as suitable for making in large quantities.

Preparation:

1. Prepare one recipe of *Basic White Fondant,* omitting vanilla and substituting almond flavoring.

2. Use as many red maraschino cherries as number of candies desired. Drain off liquid and let stand on rack to dry.

3. Pinch off small pieces of fondant and flatten between the palms. Then wrap this around each cherry. Place in refrigerator to firm for 3 to 4 hours and remove 30 minutes before dipping in Chocolate Coating.

Cherry Cordials

(Recommended as Centers for Chocolate or Summer Coating)

This is the soft type of fondant which liquefies around the cherries after they have been chocolate coated.

The night before you plan to make these cordials start the preparation. Rinse the candied cherries in a sieve under warm running water until all the preservatives and the bitter taste are removed. (This is the way the professional chocolatiers do it.) After the cherries have been thoroughly drained, cover them with brandy, kirsch, or

rum and let stand overnight in covered glass jar. Drain again before coating with fondant.

With this recipe work as quickly as possible. The addition of the chemical mixture given below (available at a pharmacy) will make these centers extremely soft, and over-handling will make them difficult to coat with chocolate.

Utensils:

1   1-quart double boiler
1   wooden spoon
1   set measuring spoons
1   set measuring cups
1   large baking sheet lined with waxed
     paper

Ingredients:

1   pound (454 grams) prepared candied
     cherries (Do not use maraschino type.)
Brandy, kirsch, or rum to cover
1½ cups (360 ml) fondant freshly made
½   ounce grain alcohol, ½ ounce glycerine,
     ½ ounce 8 percent acetic acid, and
     1 ounce distilled water—mixed by
     druggist. *Use ½ teaspoon (2.5 ml) for this
     recipe.*

Preparation:

1. The night before you plan to make these cordials prepare the cherries by rinsing them thoroughly under running water.

2. Shake off excess water, place in jar, and cover with desired liquor.For milder flavor, cover for 3 to 4 hours.

3. The next morning drain thoroughly—but do not squeeze—and place on rack to dry.

4. After drying, roll the cherries in confectioners' sugar until they are completely coated, then place them in a strainer and lightly shake off the surplus sugar.

5. Melt the fondant in top of double boiler over simmering—but not boiling—water.

6. Add ½ teaspoon (2.5 ml) of the above chemical mixture and stir until thoroughly blended.

7. Using a dipping fork, immediately coat the cherries with the fondant.

8. Place the fondant-coated cherries on a tray in the refrigerator for a few minutes to firm. Remove and immediately dip in the chocolate, or the fondant will start to liquefy and run all over the tray. Dipping these candies differs from regular chocolate dipping in that they must be double dipped. The liquefying process will take 12 hours. As the fondant liquefies it will settle to the bottom of the chocolate, and the thin layer of Chocolate Coating will not be strong enough to withstand the internal pressure of the liquid.

9. Place on waxed paper to dry and glaze over.

Store in a cool, dry place at room temperature.

Yield: About 48 cherries.

Variation:

Cherries may be replaced with plump seedless raisins or ½-inch cubes of candied pineapple.

Chapter 14
NOUGAT

Nougat is not exactly the easiest candy to prepare, and a heavy-duty mixer is a must. I tested many recipes for this book with the novice candymaker in mind.

With just a slight re-editing to conform to the style of other recipes in the book, I chose a nougat recipe taught at a turn-of-the-century cooking school. And in choosing the basic recipe, I decided on convenience instead of strict tradition. Only a purist will miss honey in the finished tender and chewy nougat. Just package the gift with a clever honey bee motif, and the recipient will never be the wiser.

Refer to *Divinity-Making Basics* (pp. 130-131) for step-by-step instructions.

Basic Nougat

(Recommended as Centers for Chocolate or Summer Coating)

Utensils:

1   2-quart heavy saucepan
1   wooden spoon
1   set measuring cups
1   set measuring spoons
Candy thermometer
Heavy-duty electric mixer
Large mixing bowl
1   loaf pan, 9 x 5 x 2 ¾ inches

Ingredients:

1½ cups (360 ml) light brown sugar, firmly packed
½   cup (120 ml) light corn syrup
½   cup (120 ml) water
1   egg white, room temperature, stiffly beaten
1   cup (240 ml) lightly roasted almonds, slivered
1   teaspoon (5 ml) vanilla
Cornstarch for coating

Preparation:

1. Lightly grease sides of saucepan.

2. Add sugar, corn syrup, and water. Cook over low heat, stirring constantly with the wooden spoon, until sugar is dissolved. You should not be able to feel sugar grains when you rub the spoon against the side of the saucepan.

3. Remove from heat and, with a damp paper towel or small sponge, wipe any remaining grains from the sides of the pan above the liquid level. Return to moderate heat.

4. Cover the pan long enough for the mixture to boil, 2 or 3 minutes—no more!

5. Uncover the pan and wipe the sides *again* to remove any stray sugar grains.

6. Start the syrup boiling again and clip on the candy thermometer.

7. Cook over low heat, without stirring, until thermometer registers 238°F. or 114°C. (syrup forms a soft ball (p. 26) in cold water).

8. Pour one-half of the hot syrup in a slow, steady stream onto the beaten egg white, beating constantly with electric mixer while you return the remaining cooked syrup to low heat and cook to 290°F. or 143°C. (syrup forms a soft crack (p. 26) in cold water).

9. Pour the second half of the hot syrup in a slow, steady stream over the egg white mixture, still beating constantly until it is thick and heavy.

10. At this point take a very small amount on a spoon. If it holds its shape when cool, and it is not sticky to the touch, it has been beaten long enough.

11. Blend in the nuts and vanilla. Pour into lightly greased loaf pan which has been dusted with cornstarch. Let stand overnight in a cool, dry place, but do not refrigerate.

12. Cut into ¾-inch by 1-inch pieces. If the nougat is not to be dipped, pieces should be wrapped in waxed paper or plastic wrap and stored in airtight container in cool, dry place.

Yield: 60 pieces

Variations:

White Nougat: Omit brown sugar and substitute sifted granulated sugar.

Gum-Drop Nougat: Omit brown sugar and substitute sifted granulated sugar. Omit almonds. Substitute 1 cup (240 ml) fruit-flavored gum drops cut into ¼-inch cubes.

Christmas Nougat: Omit brown sugar and substitute sifted granulated sugar. Omit almonds. Substitute ½ cup (120 ml) candied cherries, finely chopped.

Chapter 15
DIVINITY

This is a Kentucky specialty, but no one knows exactly when or how it arrived there. Perhaps the first divinity was made by a pioneer bride-to-be named Anne McGinty, who, according to legend, walked over the Alleghenies in 1776 with her farm animals, ducks, and chickens. Anne and other pioneer women carried treasured recipes which, when they settled, they had to adapt to the foods at hand. It might have been Anne herself who first thought to add more egg whites to lighten the heavy nougat mixture, who pronounced the confection "divine," and called the candy "divinity."

Cooking divinities was my mother's specialty. She considered a successful batch the supreme test of her kitchen skills. As soon as she poured the cooked syrup into the stiffly beaten egg whites, the five of us children would peer into the bowl, waiting for the magic moment that would determine whether the divinity would harden into fluffy peaks—or remain glossy and limp. In those days, before rural electricity, my mother had to beat the candy with a wire whisk. There was always a special excitement as she quickly dolloped the little mounds onto waxed paper. We squealed objections when we thought she was scraping the bowl too thoroughly. The candies would be taken away and hidden for a day or two to ripen, but the leavings in the bowl were ours to enjoy then and there.

Divinity-Making Basics:

You create this light-as-air relative of the nougat by boiling sugar, water, and corn syrup to the firm, or hard-ball, stage and slowly beating the hot syrup into stiffly beaten egg whites—not unlike the process for nougat. But then you either drop individual mounds from the tip of a teaspoon onto waxed paper or pour the mixture into a lightly greased pan and cut into 1-inch squares.

A word of truth is better than a ruined batch of candy and certainly less expensive in the case of divinities. The word is *weather.* To get the texture of this candy to firm—the way it *must* be—you absolutely need a clear day with low humidity and normal, steady barometric pressure. Most candy recipes are tested in climate-controlled professional kitchens where the cooks give hardly a thought to the variations in weather that a candymaker faces at home. I hereby label divinity—like most temperature-controlled candies in this book—a fair-weather confection. On a good day, the following steps will produce a light, fluffy, and creamy divinity:

Step 1: Read the recipe through in its entirety, so that nothing you need or need to do takes you by surprise. The cooking must proceed quite rapidly.

Step 2: Do not double the recipe. Beating is difficult if the recipe is too large.

Step 3: Remove the eggs you will need from the refrigerator and immediately separate the yolks from the whites. Place whites in large mixing bowl and let them come to room temperature before beating. Return the yolks to the refrigerator.

Step 4: Lightly grease sides of saucepan.

Step 5: Measure the liquid in the recipe and bring it to a full boil.

Step 6: Remove the boiling liquid from the heat; add the required sugar.

Step 7: Cover the pan long enough for the mixture to boil, which should take 2 or 3 minutes—no more! The boiling produces enough steam to wash crystals from the sides of the pan.

Step 8: As soon as the pan is uncovered, use a damp paper towel or small sponge to wipe any newly formed crystals from the sides of the pan above the liquid level.

Step 9: Make certain candy thermometer has no clinging crystals from previous use. Clip on the candy thermometer. Cook over medium-low heat, without stirring, until the correct recipe temperature is reached.

Step 10: Begin beating the egg whites when candy is almost cooked so the syrup will not have time to cool. Do *not* start beating the egg whites before you start cooking the syrup, or the foam will revert to its original liquid state and the whites then cannot be beaten again.

Step 11: Pour the syrup over the stiffly beaten egg whites in a slow, steady stream. If you can arrange to have two people work on combining the syrup and the egg whites, have one pour while the other continues to beat.

Step 12: Don't fret if the first portion of the syrup becomes hard when it meets the cooler temperature of the egg whites. As you add more syrup, the heat will soften the mixture.

Step 13: Beat divinities with a balloon whisk, electric hand mixer, or a standard electric mixer.

Step 14: Beat continuously until the mixture loses its gloss and retains its shape when dropped from a spoon.

Step 15: Work quickly when you drop the candy or it will cool in the mixing bowl.

Step 16: Remember that divinities are perishable if exposed to the air. Store in an airtight container and in a cool place. They may be frozen indefinitely.

Basic White Divinity

(Recommended as Centers for Chocolate or Summer Coating)

Utensils:

1   2-quart heavy saucepan
1   wooden spoon
1   set measuring spoons
1   set measuring cups
Balloon whisk or electric mixer
Candy thermometer
Large mixing bowl
Large baking sheet lined with waxed paper

Ingredients:

½   cup (120 ml) light corn syrup
½   cup (120 ml) water
2   cups (480 ml) granulated sugar, sifted
¼   teaspoon (1.25 ml) salt
¼   cup (60 ml) (2 large) egg whites
1   teaspoon (5 ml) vanilla
½   cup (120 ml) walnuts or pecans, chopped

Preparation:

1. Lightly grease sides of saucepan.

2. Add corn syrup and water. Cook over moderate heat until mixture boils.

3. Remove from heat; add sugar and salt.

4. Stir with wooden spoon until sugar grains

are dissolved. You should not be able to feel sugar grains when you rub the spoon against the sides of the saucepan.

5. Remove from heat and, with a damp towel or small sponge, wipe any remaining grains from the sides of the pan above the liquid level.

6. Return the mixture to moderate heat.

7. Cover the pan long enough for the mixture to boil, which should take 2 or 3 minutes—no more!

8. Uncover the pan, remove from heat, and with a damp paper towel or small sponge *again* wipe the sides of the pan above the liquid level to remove any stray sugar grains.

9. Start the syrup boiling again and clip on the candy thermometer.

10. Cook over medium-low heat, without stirring, until thermometer registers 260°F. or 127°C. (syrup forms a hard ball (p. 26) in cold water.)

11. Begin beating egg whites when candy is almost cooked so the syrup will not have time to cool. Beat until very stiff and continue beating while adding the cooked syrup in a slow, steady stream. Do *not* scrape pan. Continue beating until candy loses its gloss and will retain its shape when a sampling is dropped from a spoon onto waxed paper.

12. Add vanilla during latter part of beating.

13. Remove beaters and blend in nuts with a wooden spoon.

14. Drop by teaspoonfuls onto waxed-paper-lined baking sheet.
When cool, store in airtight container.

Yield: About 36 pieces.

Variations:

Failure-Proof Divinity: Assemble utensils and prepare ingredients as in Basic Recipe. Proceed to clipping on the candy thermometer. Cook slowly, without stirring, until thermometer registers 240°F. or 116°C. (syrup forms a soft ball (p. 26) in cold water). Begin beating egg whites when candy is almost cooked so the syrup will not have time to cool. Beat until very stiff peaks form. Remove thermometer and beat continuously while adding about one half the cooked syrup in a slow, steady stream to the beaten egg whites. Return remaining syrup to moderate heat. Again, clip on thermometer. Cook slowly, without stirring, until thermometer registers 265°F. or 129°C. (syrup forms a hard ball (p. 26) in cold water). Keep beating the first mixture while the second half of the syrup is cooking. Pour the remainder of the hot syrup in a slow, steady stream over the egg whites, beating continuously. Do *not* scrape pan. Proceed as in Basic Recipe.

Raisin-Nut Divinity: Add ½ cup (120 ml) chopped raisins. Substitute any desired flavoring.

Cherry Divinity: Omit nuts and add ½ cup (120 ml) chopped candied cherries. Tint delicate pink with food coloring.

Christmas Divinity: Omit vanilla and walnuts or pecans. Substitute ½ cup (120 ml) chopped candied cherries, ½ cup (120 ml) blanched slivered almonds, and 1 teaspoon (5 ml) almond extract.

Peppermint Divinity: Omit nuts and substitute 1 cup (240 ml) crushed peppermint stick candy.

Orange Divinity: Add 3 tablespoons (45 ml) finely grated orange rind.

Maple Divinity: Add ½ cup (120 ml) pure maple syrup to the corn syrup and water mixture. Cook over medium-low heat until

thermometer registers 265°F. or 129°C. (syrup forms a hard ball (p. 26) in cold water).

Honey Divinity: Omit corn syrup and substitute ½ cup (120 ml) strained light honey. Cook over medium-low heat, without stirring, until thermometer registers 265°F. or 129°C. (syrup forms a hard ball (p. 26) in cold water). Add 2 cups (480 ml) miniature-size marshmallows with the vanilla. This is a delicious divinity with good keeping qualities. Perfect for shipping.

Chocolate Divinity: Substitute 1 cup (240 ml) firmly packed light brown sugar and 1 cup (240 ml) sifted granulated sugar for the 2 cups (480 ml) of granulated. Add 2 squares (2 ounces or 57 grams) coarsely grated unsweetened chocolate when adding sugars and salt. Cook over medium-low heat, without stirring, until thermometer registers 265°F. or 129°C. (syrup forms a hard ball (p. 26) in cold water).

Coffee-Flavored Divinity: Omit water and substitute strong black coffee.

Dipping Divinity:

These centers can be dipped in Chocolate or Summer Coating as soon as they have cooled to room temperature. The divinity will continue to cream inside its airtight coating. I prefer these light-as-air coated confections to the more traditional fondant-coated creams.

The centers may be dipped in irregular shapes as dropped from the end of a teaspoon, or these little mounds may be formed into balls before they have completely cooled. Divinity can also be poured into a lightly greased 8 x 8 x 2 inch pan and cut into ½-inch squares.

Divinity Pastels

(Not Recommended as Centers for Coating)

A gelatin-base divinity is sometimes known as Rainbow Divinity *or* Jello Divinity. *Its prettiest virtue is that you can make it in an almost unlimited number of flavor and color combinations.*

Utensils:

1   3-quart heavy saucepan
1   wooden spoon
1   set measuring spoons
1   set measuring cups
Balloon whisk or electric mixer
Candy thermometer
Large mixing bowl
Large baking sheet lined with waxed paper

Ingredients:

¾   cup (180 ml) light corn syrup
¾   cup (180 ml) water
3   cups (720 ml) granulated sugar, sifted
¼   teaspoon (1.25 ml) salt
¼   cup (60 ml) (2 large) egg whites
3   tablespoons (45 ml) fruit-flavored gelatin, any flavor
1   cup (240 ml) nuts, chopped (optional)
¾   cup (180 ml) flaked or shredded coconut

Preparation:

1. Lightly grease sides of saucepan.

2. Add corn syrup and water. Cook over moderate heat until mixture boils.

3. Remove from heat; add sugar and salt.

4. Stir with wooden spoon until sugar is dissolved. You should not be able to feel sugar grains when you rub the spoon against the sides of the saucepan.

5. Return the mixture to moderate heat. Cover the pan long enough for the mixture to boil, which should take 2 or 3 minutes—no more!

6. Uncover the pan. Remove from heat and, with a damp paper towel or small sponge, wipe the sides of the pan above the liquid level to remove any stray sugar grains.

7. Start the syrup boiling again and clip on the candy thermometer.

8. Cook over medium-low heat, without stirring, until thermometer registers 250°F. or 121°C. (syrup forms a hard ball (p. 26) in cold water). Begin beating egg whites when candy is almost cooked so the syrup will not have time to cool. Beat until very stiff peaks form.

9. Beat continuously while adding the cooked syrup in a slow, steady stream to the beaten egg whites. Do *not* scrape pan.

10. Continue beating egg whites until soft peaks form; gradually add gelatin, beating to stiff peaks. Continue beating until candy loses its gloss and will retain its shape when a sampling is dropped from a spoon onto waxed paper.

11. Remove beaters and blend in nuts and coconut with a wooden spoon.

12. Drop by teaspoonfuls onto waxed-paper-lined baking sheets.

When cool, store in airtight container.

Yield: About 54 pieces.

Seafoam

(Recommended as Centers for Chocolate or Summer Coating)

The swirl of the beating of this candy somehow suggests sea foam. Serve it in a pearl shell candy dish if you're lucky enough to own one. If you're not so lucky, put the thought of the sea away and call the candy by one of its other names—Brown Sugar or Penuche Divinity.

Utensils:

1 3-quart heavy saucepan
1 wooden spoon
1 set measuring spoons
1 set measuring cups
Balloon whisk or electric mixer
Candy thermometer
Large mixing bowl
Large baking sheet lined with waxed paper

Ingredients:

¾ cup (180 ml) water
3 cups (720 ml) light brown sugar, firmly packed
¼ teaspoon (1.25 ml) salt
¼ cup (60 ml) (2 large) egg whites
1 teaspoon (5 ml) vanilla

Preparation:

1. Lightly grease sides of saucepan.

2. Add water, sugar, and salt. Cook over low heat, stirring constantly with the wooden spoon, until sugar is dissolved. You should not be able to feel sugar grains when you rub the spoon against the sides of the saucepan.

3. Remove from heat and, with a damp paper towel or small sponge, wipe any remaining grains from the sides of the pan above the liquid level.

4. Return the mixture to moderate heat. Cover the pan long enough for the mixture to boil, which should take 2 or 3 minutes—no more!

5. Uncover the pan and *again* wipe the sides above the liquid level to remove any stray sugar grains. This step is a *must*.

6. Start the syrup boiling again and clip on the candy thermometer.

7. Cook over low heat, without stirring, until thermometer registers 255°F. or 124°C. (syrup forms a hard ball (p. 26) in cold water).

8. Begin beating egg whites when candy is almost cooked so the syrup will not have time to cool. Beat until very stiff peaks form.

9. Beat continuously while adding the cooked syrup in a slow, steady stream to the beaten egg whites. Do *not* scrape pan.

10. Continue beating until candy loses its gloss and retains its shape when a sampling is dropped from a spoon onto waxed paper. Add vanilla during latter part of beating.

11. Drop by teaspoonfuls onto waxed-paper-lined baking sheet.

When cool, store in a cool, dry place in air-tight container.

Yield: About 54 pieces.

Chapter 16
CRYSTALLINE CANDIES

These are lollipops and the classic hard clear candies in vivid colors that glitter through the glass of a candy-store window.

In making hard candies, the trick is to avoid too much crystallization, which will dull them. To insure clarity and brightness, I use large amounts of corn syrup and less sugar.

Professional candymakers add citric acid to give their candies a sharp, tangy flavor. This white, water-soluble powder does not withstand high cooking temperatures so you must fold it into the candy mass only after you have poured the syrup onto a baking sheet and it has cooled for two to three minutes. It is wiser for the at-home candy cook to skip citric acid and use strong flavoring oils to intensify the flavors. (See Sources of Supply, p. 217.)

Crystalline Candy-Making Basics:

Step 1: Measure and bring the liquid in the recipe to a full boil in a deep rather than wide pan so the syrup will not spread over too large a surface and darken too much while it cooks. The upper part of a 2-quart double boiler is a good shape and size.

Step 2: Remove the boiling liquid from the heat and add the sugar. Stir until sugar grains are dissolved. With a damp paper towel or small sponge, wipe any stray grains from the sides of the pan above the liquid level. If the sugar grains are not dissolved (you can tell if you feel grains when you stir with a wooden spoon), return the mixture to very low heat. But under no circumstances let it boil again or the sugar grains will multiply, producing a grainy hard candy. Repeat the wiping process as above and make sure no crystals fall into the mixture.

Step 3: Return the syrup to moderate heat. Clip on the candy thermometer before mixture boils. Do not move the thermometer after syrup has come to a boil at 300°F. or 149°C. Any slight movement can cause over-crystallization.

Step 4: Remove the cooked syrup from the heat and cool to approximately 160°F. or 71°C. Add the flavoring oil and color. See Coloring and Flavoring Charts (pp. 30-31). Use a large amount of flavoring oil because the high temperature of the syrup causes some of the essence to evaporate.

Step 5: Work rapidly as soon as you stir the flavoring and coloring into the hot syrup because you have cooked the mixture at a high temperature and it will harden quickly.

Step 6: Do not try to cut hard candies into perfect squares. Leave that trick to professionals. Instead pour the syrup into a lightly greased square pan, small molds, toy muffin tins, or drop it from a small spoon in 1-inch dollops. If the syrup gets too firm for spooning, reheat over very low heat.

Step 7: Wrap individual crystalline candies in waxed paper or plastic wrap. Unwrapped, they become sticky in hot or humid weather. They keep best stored in an airtight container.

Sugarcoat hard candies if you do not wish to wrap them. Coating will prevent their sticking together, and you will be able to keep them a longer time as a decorative candy.

Step 1: To sugarcoat candies, thoroughly dampen a lint-free tea towel (just damp, not wet). Place candies on one-half of the towel, making certain they are separated; then fold over the second half of the damp towel for a few seconds. The candies should be just sticky and not wet.

Step 2: Dip each sticky candy in a bowl of granulated sugar and place them on racks to dry. Package them in clear plastic bags and tie with colorful ribbon.

Spiced Hard Candy

(Not Recommended as Centers for Coating)

In Greencastle, Indiana, my home town, the local daily newspaper sponsors an annual Cook Book Contest. Contestants submit recipes and the paper publishes them in a special 25-page supplement. Believe me, it is all very professional, with special categories and prizes for "Best Recipe of Its Kind." Since everyone in the county follows the contest, no one would think of letting her name appear with a recipe until she was absolutely sure it was superior. For instance, the following—which was judged best of its kind in 1972.

Utensils:

1 2-quart pan with deep sides
1 wooden spoon
1 set measuring spoons
1 set measuring cups
Candy thermometer
1 mallet
1 pan, 8 x 8 x 2 inches

Ingredients:

1 cup (240 ml) light corn syrup
½ cup (120 ml) water
2 cups (480 ml) granulated sugar, sifted
1 teaspoon (5 ml) oil of cinnamon, peppermint, spearmint, wintergreen, anise, orange or lemon. (Use less, if desired.)
¼ teaspoon (1.25 ml) food coloring

Preparation:

1. Lightly grease sides of pan.

2. Add corn syrup and water. Cook over low heat, stirring constantly with a wooden spoon, until sugar is dissolved. You should not be able to feel sugar grains when you rub the spoon against the sides of the pan.

3. Remove from heat and, with a damp paper towel or small sponge, wipe any remaining grains from the sides of the pan above the liquid level.

4. Clip on the candy thermometer and start syrup boiling. Cook over moderate heat, without stirring, until thermometer registers 300°F. or 149°C. (syrup forms a hard crack (p. 26) in cold water). The last twenty degrees of cooking should be done over low heat.

5. Remove from heat and cool syrup to 160°F. or 71°C.

6. Stir in flavoring oil and food coloring, see Flavoring and Coloring Charts, pp. 30-31. Immediately pour into lightly greased pan or molds, or drop from tip of small spoon onto baking sheet. Do *not* scrape pan.

7. Cool. Turn out onto smooth surface and break into eating-size pieces with mallet. Sugarcoat, if desired.

8. Store in airtight container with pieces separated in layers between sheets of waxed paper.

Yield: Approximately 1¼ pounds (568 grams).

Variations:

Dropped Lollipop Patties: Use the preceding recipe for Spiced Hard Candy. The rest is easy. Choose a food color to go with the flavor. See Coloring and Flavoring Charts, pp. 30-31. Check weather; a humid day is not good for making lollipops. Dampness causes the candies to become moist and sticky.

Prepare baking sheet by brushing well with vegetable oil. Have lollipop sticks on the oiled baking sheet ready to receive patties. From this point work must be done very rapidly because the syrup has been cooked to a high temperature and will harden quickly. For small flat lollipops, drop syrup from the tip of a tablespoon onto sticks. The surface must be level or the lollipops will not be round. If decorations such as gumdrops or cut-up pieces of marshmallow are to be used, they should be placed on the candy while it is still warm, so they will stick to the surface. For large lollipops, pour the syrup directly from the pan onto the sticks. Let the lollipops cool until just barely warm to the fingers and then loosen them from the baking sheet, using a wide spatula. If allowed to remain until hard they will crack when being removed.

Yield: 30 small or 20 large lollipops.

Chapter 17
CANDIED POPCORN

Candied popcorn confection evolved from the frontier custom of popping corn to use as breakfast cereal. Sweetened with molasses and covered with rich milk, this tasty breakfast was very much enjoyed by young and old.

It was only natural to start boiling the molasses and milk together into a candied syrup to pour over the popped corn.

Besides being delicious, nutritious, and inexpensive, candied popcorn has the great virtue of adapting to any shape or form you wish to fashion. You can make it into enormous table decorations, tiny favors for children's parties, or a deliciousness of abstraction to sell for quick and easy profit at benefits and bazaars.

Two cups (480 ml) of unpopped corn will make nine cups popped corn, allowing for discards of unpopped kernels.

Popcorn-Making Basics:

Step 1: Unless you use the wire-basket method—in which you just shake the popcorn a few inches over a flame—or an electric popcorn popper, you need to use a saucepan with a heavy bottom as it distributes the heat best. You also need a lid that will keep the corn in and let the steam escape or you will end up with soggy popcorn.

Step 2: Peanut oil cooks just right. Never use butter or margarine: they smoke and burn at 420°F. or 216°C., the temperature at which the corn pops.

Step 3: Heat oil to cover bottom of pan for a few minutes, then drop in a few kernels. When they pop, you're ready to go.

Step 4: Toss in enough kernels to cover the bottom of the pan. Cover loosely enough to let the steam escape and, when the popping starts, shake gently but constantly until it's done.

Step 5: When the popping stops, take from the heat and uncover. Turn into large mixing bowl. Pop 1¼ cups (300 ml) of uncooked popcorn to measure 9 cups (2160 ml).

Step 6: Keep popcorn warm in 250°F. or 121°C. oven while preparing the syrup.

Step 2: Put the popped corn into a large mixing bowl so there will be plenty of room to stir the corn while the syrup is being added.

Step 3: Prepare any of the three syrups suggested on pp. 140-144.

Step 4: When the syrup is removed from the heat, pour it over the warm popcorn, stirring very gently with a wooden spoon until the corn is well coated.

Step 5. When you are sure the corn is cool enough to handle with lightly buttered fingers, press it into balls or any of the forms suggested on pp. 142-143. (I wear rubber gloves and work while the candied corn is still quite warm because it is then much easier to mold.) When working with large quantities, pour the hot syrup over only a portion of the popped corn at a time and form balls from this. Set the pan containing the remainder of the syrup in a pan of hot water until ready to use. In this way the syrup will not have a chance to cool and harden before the balls can be shaped. In forming popcorn balls use as little pressure as possible so the kernels will not be crushed. Any dry, ready-to-eat cereal may be substituted for popped corn.

Yield: 9 cups (2160 ml) popped candied corn will make fifteen balls 2½ inches in diameter.

Candied Popcorn Basics:

Step 1: Use only the large, well-popped kernels. Sort and reject hard pieces of corn that have not completely popped. A small amount of salt put on the popped corn will add to the flavor of the balls, but do not use nearly so much as when the popped corn is to be served with butter. A very light sprinkling is recommended.

Vanilla Sugar Syrup

Utensils:

1   2-quart heavy saucepan
1   wooden spoon
1   set measuring spoons
1   set measuring cups
Candy thermometer

Ingredients:

2 tablespoons (30 ml) light corn syrup
1¼ cups (300 ml) water
2 cups (480 ml) granulated sugar, sifted
Food coloring (optional)
1 teaspoon (5 ml) vanilla

Preparation:

1. Lightly grease sides of saucepan.

2. Add corn syrup, water, and sugar. Cook over low heat, stirring constantly with the wooden spoon, until sugar is dissolved. You should not be able to feel sugar grains when you rub the spoon against the sides of the saucepan.

3. Remove from heat and, with a damp paper towel or small sponge, wipe any remaining grains from the sides of the saucepan above the liquid level.

4. Return to moderate heat. Cover the pan long enough for the mixture to boil, which should take 2 or 3 minutes—no more!

5. Uncover the pan and *again* wipe the sides above the liquid level to remove any stray sugar grains.

6. Start the syrup boiling again and clip on the candy thermometer.

7. Cook over low heat, without stirring, until thermometer registers 290°F. or 143°C. (syrup forms a soft crack (p. 26) in cold water).

8. Remove from heat and stir in food coloring and the vanilla. (If you choose to use food coloring, it will take a large amount to counteract the basic white of the popped corn.)

9. Pour hot syrup over warm popcorn and stir with wooden spoon to blend.

Yield: Enough to cover 9 cups popped corn or fifteen balls 2½ inches in diameter.

Old-Fashioned Molasses Syrup

Utensils:

1 2-quart heavy saucepan
1 wooden spoon
1 set measuring spoons
1 set measuring cups
Candy thermometer

Ingredients:

1 cup (240 ml) light molasses
1 cup (240 ml) dark corn syrup
1 tablespoon (15 ml) cider vinegar
3 tablespoons (45 ml) butter

Preparation:

1. Lightly grease sides of saucepan.

2. Add molasses, corn syrup, and vinegar. Cook over low heat, stirring constantly.

3. When the syrup starts boiling clip on the candy thermometer.

4. Cook slowly, stirring occasionally. Move the candy thermometer around to prevent syrup from scorching. After 240°F. or 116°C. is reached, more frequent stirring is necessary. Continue cooking until thermometer registers 290°F. or 143°C. (syrup forms a soft crack (p. 26) in cold water).

5. Remove from heat, add butter, and stir with wooden spoon only enough to blend.

Yield: Enough to cover 9 cups popped corn or fifteen balls 2½ inches in diameter.

Marshmallow Syrup

Utensils:

1   2-quart heavy saucepan
1   wooden spoon
1   set measuring spoons
1   set measuring cups
Candy thermometer

Ingredients:

¼   cup (60 ml) butter
40 large-size marshmallows, or 4 cups
      (960 ml) miniature-size
Food coloring (optional)

Preparation:

1. Melt butter in saucepan over low heat.

2. Add marshmallows and cook, stirring constantly with the wooden spoon, until marshmallows are melted and mixture is syrupy. Stir in food coloring..

3. Pour warm syrup over warm popcorn and stir with wooden spoon to blend.

Yield: Enough to cover 9 cups popped corn or fifteen balls 2½ inches in diameter.

Variations:

(Not Recommended as Centers For Coating)

These candies can make cute decorations for any holiday party, which the children can take home as edible favors. Follow *Popcorn Making Basics* (p. 140), using whichever cooked syrup you prefer.

Christmas-Tree Popcorn Balls: It was the custom in days of old to hide a small trinket in the center of the popcorn ball as an added treat for the lucky recipient. With a long darning needle put a cord through the middle of the warm ball, wrap in plastic wrap to hang on the tree.

Surprise Balls: Shape warm candied popcorn around surprise center of a gumdrop, candied cherry, miniature marshmallow, raisin, walnut or pecan half, pitted date, or any other edible treat. Do not make these too large. Roll in colored sugar, granulated fruit gelatin, or flaked coconut.

Yield: About twenty 1½-inch balls.

Snowmen: Shape warm candied popcorn to form three balls of decreasing size for each snowman. When cool, put balls together with thick confectioners' sugar frosting. Give the snowmen cock-eyed hats with a brim from the slice of a large gumdrop and the crown a miniature gumdrop. Make eyes, nose, and mouth with raisins and cinnamon candies.

Yield: Six snowmen.

Toy Animals: Press warm candied popcorn into buttered shallow pans in a layer about ½ inch thick. When slightly cooled, cut into desired shapes with cookie cutters. Use frosting tube to decorate.

Yield: Nine toy animals.

Popcorn Bars: Press warm candied popcorn onto lightly buttered cookie sheet in a rectangle approximately 1 inch thick. Let stand until almost cool to the hands. Cut into bars approximately 1 inch wide and 3 inches long. These may be made into bricks using milk cartons, if desired. Wrap in plastic wrap for gift giving.

Yield: Nine popcorn bars.

Mr. Owl: Form five 2½-inch candied popcorn balls for the bodies of the owls. Form five smaller balls for the heads. Press the heads onto the bodies while the balls are still warm. To make wings, cut candy orange slices in half lengthwise; press two pieces in place on each body. You might have to use toothpicks to hold these in place. Cut licorice strings to form a chevron on each head. This is the mark that makes the owl look so wise—or so cross! Make eyes of orange-flavored candy circles, centered with whole cloves for pupils.

Yield: 5 owls.

Miss Pussy Cat: Form ten 4-inch candied popcorn balls. We are making just pussy-cat heads. To make ears, cut candy orange slices in half crosswise and press pieces in place on balls. Make eyes and nose of jelly beans. Use colored toothpicks for my lady's whiskers. Tie pretty bows to the ring base. Use napkin rings as holders or make your own by pasting paper strips together in circles. If the paper is used the pussy cats can serve as informal place cards with fun names for table identification. Don't get carried away with pussy-cat personalities.

Yield: 10 pussy cats.

Popcorn Tree: Double recipe for Vanilla Sugar Syrup (pp. 140-141) and use 9 (2160 ml) cups white popped corn (about 1¼ cup (300 ml) unpopped). Follow *Popcorn Making Basics* (p. 140). Divide popped corn into two large mixing bowls. Pour half the cooked syrup over the white popped corn, color the remaining portion any desired shade and pour this over the second bowl. Butter hands slightly and shape white popcorn mixture into 2-inch balls. Shape colored popcorn into fifteen 2½-inch balls. Add food coloring to 1 package (3 ounces or 85 grams) fruit-flavored gelatin in the same shade as the colored popcorn balls. Use a 10-ounce (284 gram) package of large-size marshmallows and a 10-ounce one of miniature size. Shake gelatin and coloring together in jar or use blender. Dip the marshmallows quickly in cold water and

then roll in the colored gelatin. Place on racks to dry.

To Assemble Tree: On a large flat plate or foil-covered cardboard, arrange a circle of eleven of the colored balls, securing one to the other with toothpicks. Fill in center with 7 white balls. Pyramid remaining balls, alternating colors; continue to fill in centers with white balls. If desired, omit top ball and carefully insert candy canes tied with a colorful bow, or any other appropriate decoration. Tuck colored marshmallows among the balls of popcorn. This gives a lovely effect.

Molded Popcorn Decorations: For individual forms use a one- or two-piece mold, well buttered or oiled. Cake molds or foil molds from the supermarket can be used. Press the candied popcorn into all the corners and curves. When cold, lift out carefully and decorate as desired.

Old-Fashioned Molasses-Peanut Popcorn

(Not Recommended as Centers for Coating)

Red and blue boxes of Cracker Jack are as American as apple pie and the Fourth of July, but homemade Cracker Jack may well be crisper and crunchier. Make your own for children's parties or a summer picnic treat. Package the clusters in plastic bags and tie a trinket to the outside with a gay red and blue ribbon.

Preparation:

1. Prepare 9 cups (2160 ml) popped corn and one recipe of *Old-Fashioned Molasses Syrup* (p. 141). Roast 2 cups (480 ml) peanuts with skins in oven. See p. 28 for method.

2. Remove the cooked syrup from heat and quickly add the peanuts.

3. Take the popcorn out of the oven and add the syrup a little at a time, stirring gently, but continuously, with a wooden spoon. Incorporate the syrup quickly, or else it will become too brittle.

4. When all the syrup is mixed with the popcorn, spread it out on a foil-lined smooth surface. Separate candied corn into small clusters. As soon as it is cool, pack in plastic bags.

Store in cool, dry place. Do not place in refrigerator or freeze. Will keep approximately 2 weeks.

Yield: Approximately 3 quarts (2880 ml).

Buttered Caramel Corn Crunch

(Not Recommended as Centers for Coating)

Buttered caramel popcorn is sold in almost every confectionery store under various trade names. It is usually packaged in 1-quart containers and is quite expensive compared to the cost of making your own. I keep 1-pound coffee tins for this purpose, and cover them with self-adhesive gift paper to make very attractive containers. This confection is an excellent choice to make in quantity for gift giving, benefit sales, or bazaars.

Preparation:

1. Prepare 9 cups (2160 ml) popped corn and one recipe for Caramel Coating (pp. 184-185). Use 1 cup (240 ml) large pecan pieces, unroasted, and 1 cup (240 ml) whole roasted almonds. See p. 28 for roasting method.

2. Add the nuts to the popcorn and place in slow oven (250°F. or 121°C.).

3. Cook syrup until a small quantity dropped into cold water forms a soft crack (p. 26).

4. Remove the popcorn mixture from the oven and add the syrup a little at a time, stirring gently, but continuously, with a wooden spoon.

5. When all the syrup is mixed with the popcorn mixture, spread it out on a foil-lined smooth surface. Separate crunch into small clusters. As soon as it is cool, pack in plastic bags.

Store in cool, dry place. Do not place in refrigerator or freeze. Will keep for 4 to 6 weeks.

Yield: Approximately 3 quarts (2880 ml).

CANDY COATING
AND DIPPING

Embellishing candy centers by dipping them in a delicious chocolate coating is the epitome of the art of home candy-making.

The previous chapters in this book are intended to be a complete and practical collection of recipes for the at-home candy cook, presenting easy-to-follow step-by-step instructions. Each recipe indicates whether or not it is recommended as a dipping center.

Nothing, but nothing, will impress your dinner guests more than a presentation of richly coated chocolates with strong after-dinner coffee. Mastering the easy technique of chocolate dipping will guarantee you a ready gift from your kitchen. An assortment of the chocolates in this chapter, creatively packaged, make an excellent fund raiser—especially appealing to people of discriminating taste and the means to indulge themselves.

Chapter 18
EASY-METHOD
CHOCOLATE DIPPING

This chapter introduces a new and revolutionary method for hand coating chocolates of a professional quality.

Seven years of home testing my easy method have convinced me that anyone with the willingness to try can quickly learn the art of chocolate dipping.

The mystique of coating chocolates should not intimidate anybody. With a few simple kitchen tools and two supermarket ingredients, you will soon be thrilled to discover that you, too, can make extravagant-looking confections that are as elegant as any that can be purchased from an expensive chocolatier.

Custom-blending your own mixture will enable you to make batch after batch of firm and glossy milk or dark chocolates without the slightest blemish or gray streak to betray the amateur hand.

Purchasing of Ingredients:

Use an unsweetened (or bitter) pure chocolate that comes in eight-ounce packages from the supermarket. (I use Baker's.) This is the natural rich chocolate ground from cocoa beans and it contains cocoa butter. Read the list of ingredients on the package label carefully. If it states that vegetable shortening is included in the ingredients—do not use it. It is the cocoa butter in the pure chocolate that gives the finished chocolates their glossy sheen and mouth-watering rich taste. You would have to add cocoa butter to a chocolate that contains vegetable shortening, and this technique belongs in the hands of professionals. I do not use the semisweet block chocolate because this adds too much sweetness to the chocolate coating and obscures its taste.

The other ingredient is summer (white) coating. This import from Switzerland is sold under various brand names, including Rose Crest, Suchaard, and Nestlés. It contains sugar, vegetable fat, dry whole milk, nonfat dry milk, lecithin, flavoring, and salt. (Lecithin is the ingredient that keeps the chocolate mixture fluid.) It will automatically stabilize the chocolate mixture. In plain culinary language this simply means that the cocoa butter will not separate from the rest of

the ingredients and cause those hated gray streaks.

If summer coating is unavailable in your local supermarket, it can be purchased in bulk from a candy store where it is usually labeled "white chocolate." This is a misnomer because chocolate must contain cocoa butter to be legally sold as such. *Do not substitute imported white chocolate candy bars;* these do not contain enough of the necessary lecithin. (See Sources of Supply p. 218 for ordering white coating.)

Weather Conditions and Chocolate Dipping:

Avoid dipping chocolates in a draft; they will dry with gray streaks. The basic mixture of chocolate and summer coating is much less sensitive to humidity and heat than the mixture used by professional candymakers. However, there are limitations. I do not dip chocolates when the temperature is over 85°F. (29°C.), or when the humidity is over 80 percent. Of course, the weather will be of no importance if you are working in a climate-controlled kitchen. Always keep the work area free from steam or cooking vapors.

Preparation of Centers:

Individual recipes in this book give instructions for forming centers for dipping. Nuts, dried fruits, and pretzels are easier to dip than cream centers; hence it is recommended that the beginner practice with these until the hand control of dipping is mastered. Lightly roasting nuts (except pecans and walnuts) in the oven will greatly improve the flavor of the finished confection. With a little practice you will soon find yourself progressing to soft cream centers, Easter eggs, candy bars, and cookies. Indulge your imagination! Dipping with chocolate is one of the most creative of kitchen crafts.

Helpful Hints:

1. Cooked fondants must be made at least two days before you dip. If centers are freshly made before you coat with chocolate, most will have leaky bottoms within a few hours after dipping.

2. Do not dip cold centers because they will cool the chocolate mixture too fast. This will cause gray streaking. Let *all* centers stand at room temperature for several hours before dipping to dry and glaze over the surfaces.

3. Try to keep centers uniform in size and not too large—not more than ¾ inch in diameter. The Chocolate Coating will double their size.

Recommended Centers:

(See index for candy recipes.)

Cooked and Uncooked Fondants
Marzipan
Fudge
Nougat
Toffee
Butter Crunch
Dried-Fruit Confections
Divinity
Marshmallows
Jellies
Caramels
Soft Butterscotch
Easter Egg Centers
Candy Bar Centers
Cookies, graham crackers, pretzels, fresh strawberries, and orange sections can also be coated with chocolate.

Preparation of Ingredients:

Both chocolate and summer coating melt faster when finely grated by hand. (I now use my electric food processor or Oster Food Crafter.) *Caution:* Do not use an electric blender because the heat from the motor shaft will melt the chocolate prematurely and

gray streaks will appear in the final product. When grating chocolate or summer coating, be sure the grater is completely dry. Handle both as little as possible to prevent them from absorbing moisture from your hands. Work as quickly as possible. Hand-grating chocolate is a pesty chore because the flakes tend to fly around. I place the hand grater in the middle of a large bowl.

The selection of milk, dark, or bittersweet chocolate coating does not necessarily depend on the center. This is very much a matter of individual taste. Normally, the sweeter the center, the darker the chocolate coating.

Custom-Blending Dipping Chocolate:

(Four cups (960 ml) of grated mixture will coat approximately sixty ¾-inch centers.)

¼ pound (114 grams) summer coating or bitter chocolate will equal 1 cup (240 ml) finely grated.

To Prepare a Milk-Type Chocolate Coating:
3 cups (720 ml) grated summer coating
1 cup (240 ml) grated unsweetened (bitter) chocolate

To Prepare a Dark Chocolate Coating:
2 cups (480 ml) grated summer coating
2 cups (480 ml) grated unsweetened (bitter) chocolate

To Prepare a Bittersweet Chocolate Coating:
1 cup (240 ml) grated summer coating
3 cups (720 ml) grated unsweetened (bitter) chocolate

You can vary these proportions to taste, but don't use less than 1 cup summer coating to 3 cups chocolate, or the mixture will harden too fast and require frequent reheating. It is impractical to work with less than four cups of dipping mixture. You need a certain depth of coating in the pan to dip and cover the centers. I have included delicious recipes for end-of-the-pan coating.

Preparing the Work Area:

The work area should be large enough to hold a tray of centers to be dipped at one end and a baking sheet lined with waxed paper for receiving the chocolates at the other end. In the middle there must be room for the dipper to work. (See illustration below)

Utensils:

1   1-quart double boiler
Wide rubber spatula
2-cup measure
1-tablespoon measure
Hand grater
Candy thermometer (optional)
2   baking sheets lined with waxed paper

A word of caution about mixing the ingredients: Summer coating, chocolate, and water do not mix. Water thickens melted ingredients and even a tiny drop will cause trouble. If you are using a candy thermometer to test the temperature of the water in the bottom part of the double boiler while the melting mixture is nearby, be extra careful not to let any droplets fall into the mixture. Any moisture from air or from the steam of a double boiler makes the mixture crumbly and impossible to handle.

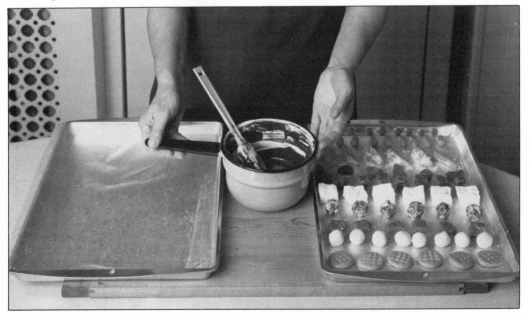

Blending Chocolate Mixture:

Put grated summer coating in top half of double boiler; put water in lower half. Do not let top half actually touch water. Bring water *almost* to boil, then stir summer coating continuously with a wide rubber spatula until it has melted. Remove pan of summer coating from over the hot water. Place candy thermometer in hot water and let the mixture cool to about 140°F. (60°C.). continue to stir summer coating until the mixture has cooled to lukewarm, about 110°F. (43°C.).

Add grated chocolate, a tablespoon (15 ml) at a time to lukewarm summer coating. Stir continuously with rubber spatula. Stirring helps homogenize and blend the cocoa butter and insures a rich, glossy sheen on the finished chocolates. If necessary, reheat the mixture over the hot water in the bottom of the double boiler for a few seconds—just long enough to melt the chocolate. Again, be careful of moisture falling into the chocolate mixture. Cool mixture to about 100°F. (38°C.), stirring constantly with rubber spatula. With a little practice you will instinctively be controlling the dipping

temperature. However, here is an infallible guide: After melted chocolate coating is thoroughly blended, place a lid over the bottom part of the double boiler containing the hot water. Set aside. Keep stirring the chocolate mixture until it is cool to the touch. It will look something like thick chocolate pudding and a string of chocolate about 1 ½ inches long will dangle from the end of the rubber spatula (See illustration.) Start making little dabs of chocolate on a separate piece of waxed paper. When the samples of wet chocolate dry and gloss over in about 1 ½ minutes, the chocolate is at the correct temperature for dipping the centers.

Leave the rubber spatula in the pan and place the melted chocolate in the middle of the prepared work area. Stir the chocolate mixture occasionally during the dipping process.

Hand-Dipping:

You will be hand-dipping directly from the pan. If you have previously used a dipping fork, you will soon learn that by hand-dipping many of your dipping problems will be solved. First, it is much easier to control the temperature by actually getting "the feel" of the mixture. Second, the excess coating, which causes the heavy bottoms on chocolates dipped with a fork, can be controlled by using the middle and index fingers of your right hand as a dipping fork. The following carefully illustrated steps outline the correct method for hand-dipping directly from the pan.

Hand-Dipping vs. Dipping Fork:

Hand-dipping is easy for the amateur. However, if you are clever with the dipping fork and would rather not change your method, refer to the illustrations using the dipping fork for coating bonbons. (See pp. 179-182.)

Step 1: With palm facing you, hold up the middle and index fingers of your right hand in a "V"-for-victory sign.

Step 2: Enclose your thumb and the rest of your fingers. The two extended fingers form the "V" for your dipping fork.

Step 3: Throughout the dipping process the left hand must be kept clean and free from chocolate in order to decorate the chocolates with nuts, sprinkles, etc. With the clean left hand, drop a center from the tray on the left side of your work area into the chocolate.

Step 4: Place the right hand formed in the "V" dipping position, into the chocolate mixture and roll the center over to coat.

Step 5: With the fingers still in the "V" position, palm side up, scoop up the coated center, which will have quite a lot of chocolate sticking to it.

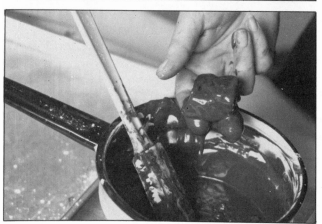

Step 6: With the coated center resting in the fork of the middle and index fingers, gently rap the backs of your fingers on the edge of the pan to make the excess chocolate flow back into the pan. This eliminates the heavy bottoms of coated chocolates— the true sign of an amateur dipper.

Step 7: Turn coated chocolate over onto tray lined with waxed paper on the right-hand side of your work area. Be careful not to slide the center around once you have deposited it on the waxed paper. This will wipe the chocolate off the bottom.

Step 8: If center does not drop easily because of stickiness, manipulate it with middle fingertip to rest against thumb and push it off.

Step 9: After coated center is placed on waxed paper, lift middle finger straight up, pulling string of chocolate with which to form fancy design.

Coated centers must be decorated immediately after they are dipped.

Reheating of Chocolate Dipping Mixture:

The mixture should remain at dipping temperature for 20 to 25 minutes, depending on variables: the weight of the metal in the double boiler, the temperature of the room, and how much "swishing" around of the chocolate mixture takes place during the dipping. The warm water in the bottom of the double boiler is less dense and cools faster than the thicker chocolate mixture. Therefore, after the chocolate mixture has cooled and become too thick for hand-dipping it may be necessary to reheat the water before reheating the chocolate mixture. There is no limit to how many times the mixture may be reheated over warm water. Just take care that the temperature of the mixture is not over 110°F. (43°C.). If chocolate is melted at too high a temperature, it most likely will not melt smoothly and may produce a grainy, undesirable coating.

If the weather conditions are favorable, you will find that by the time you have dipped a dozen or so chocolates the first will be dry and nicely glazed over. Do not panic if the coating does not seem to be drying fast enough. It will take longer on days when the temperature and humidity are higher than normal.

Step 10: After all the centers have been dipped, touch up any bare spots on the finished chocolates with a bit of chocolate on the end of the finger.

Step 11: If you have reached this step and your chocolates are still not glazing over, put the trays of dipped chocolates into the refrigerator for a very few minutes. Remove them quickly or they will sweat, and the moisture will create the gray streaks. If your chocolates dry gray-streaked despite all your efforts (and this should not happen), convert them into French creams by redipping and rolling at once in chocolate sprinkles, ground nuts, or unsweetened cocoa. In fact with unsweetened cocoa, if you dipped fudge centers originally, you will have acceptable French truffles.

How to Use Leftover Dipping Chocolate:

Remelt chocolate and mix in nuts, raisins, toasted coconut, chopped dried fruits, or chopped marshmallows—enough to use up most of the chocolate; drop mixture from a teaspoon onto waxed paper. Don't be surprised if these tasty end-of-the-pot creations turn out to be requested favorites.

Chocolate Almond Bark: Stir ¾ cup (180 ml) lightly roasted almonds into 1 cup (240 ml) leftover melted chocolate. Spread on clean baking sheet with a wide spatula to a depth of about ¼ inch and cool until firm. Break into eating-size pieces. To make the chocolate look more like bark, it may be scored with the tines of a fork before it has set. Any kind of nuts, or a combination of nuts and raisins, may be used.

Caring for Finished Chocolates:

Leave coated centers on waxed paper until the bottoms are thoroughly dry—several hours. If they are removed too soon, the chocolate may stick to the waxed paper and candies with soft centers will develop leaks. Store chocolates in single layers in airtight containers in a cool, dry place, never in direct sunlight. *Easy-Method Chocolates* do not contain preservatives. Therefore, their storage time is limited to two weeks at room temperature, or indefinitely if frozen in airtight wrapping. For gift-wrapping ideas, see The Candy Store, pp. 193-216.

CHAPTER 19
PROFESSIONAL CHOCOLATE DIPPING

My sister and I have been dipping chocolates for several years for both gift giving and a handsome profit, using our own blend of *Easy-Method* dipping chocolate, always with excellent results. However, when Tom Kron, a well-known New York chocolatier, offered a course in chocolate dipping, I enrolled. Mr. Kron is one of the few candymakers who actually does hand-dipping. Though most commercial chocolates are dipped by mechanical methods, the very best are still hand-dipped, and that means really by hand and not with a dipping fork. A young Hungarian immigrant, Mr. Kron is a chocolatier in the truest family tradition, and a knowl-edgeable teacher who is able to convey the secrets of the trade to his students. When I studied with Mr. Kron, it was indeed an education to watch a professional assistant of his, a lady aged ninety, dip chocolates with an almost alarming speed and efficiency, picking up a string of chocolate with thumb and forefinger, and embossing curlicues on the candies to distinguish one type of center from another.

Mr. Kron begins his classes by introducing the cocoa bean as the origin of the pure chocolate we use for chocolate dipping. All the different kinds of chocolate result from the varied treatment given to the cocoa beans at the processing plants. The cocoa beans, removed from the pods and cured like coffee beans, are cleaned, roasted, and crushed. The particles of crushed beans (nibs) are then put into heated grinders. The resulting thick liquid, when poured into molds, produces the regular pure baking chocolate sold at the supermarket. Sometimes it is processed further for greater smoothness. To make cocoa powder much of the cocoa butter is removed during the grinding. To make sweet, or semisweet, chocolate coating some of the cocoa butter removed in the cocoa-making process is added to the bitter chocolate along with sugar and flavoring—vanilla, or—for the continental taste—cinnamon or other spices. To make milk chocolate, milk solids are added along with the sugar. (With the *Easy-Method* the summer coating contains most of these ingredients.)

Chocolatiers are usually introduced to the carefully guarded secrets of their art by early apprenticeship in a family business that passes from generation to generation. Trained to keep permanent mental tapes of such details as soil, sun, rainfall, and maturity of the crop at particular cocoa plantations, they are connoisseurs of the quality of cocoa beans and can reel off good and bad years almost more quickly than they can recite cocoa prices on the commodities exchange.

Each family of chocolatiers has its own recipe for blending chocolate. Most recipes begin with 40 percent cocoa butter; the guarded part is the exact proportion of sugar, milk solids, and flavoring in the other 60 percent, which produces the subtle variations in the taste of fine chocolates.

In Europe, some families still mix their own blend of dipping chocolate. In the United States, the chocolatier usually sends his formula to a wholesaler, who returns the prepared chocolate in block form. The chocolatier grates and remelts the block into dipping chocolate.

Caution: For professional dipping do not attempt to blend your own mixture with summer (white) coating and grated unsweetened chocolate as in the *Easy-Method* dipping. You must use a marble slab or formica for *Professional Chocolate Dipping*, and the *Easy-Method* mixture will cool too fast if not kept in the top part of the double boiler. If you try to mix the two methods, you will have nothing but trouble with all the scraping and reheating of the chocolate mixture.

Purchasing Chocolate:

Several varieties of block chocolate can be used in this method: Semisweet (or candy-making) chocolate—available in squares. It is processed with a low viscosity to make it more fluid. It also has a satin gloss. Both these qualities make it especially good for professional dipping. Sweet cooking chocolate (German's Sweet)—available in four-ounce (114 grams) bars. Milk chocolate—available in ten-pound (4540 grams) slabs but usually sold in broken pieces in candy stores. Best of all, the regular sweet coating chocolate, which comes in ten-pound (4540 grams) cakes. It is available in any confectioners' supply house and sold in four types, varying from milk to bittersweet. (See Sources of Supply, p. 218.)

Do not use semisweet chocolate bits. These morsels are formulated to retain their shape to some extent in cookie baking. Therefore, it is almost impossible to melt them at the low temperatures recommended for dipping.

Never use less than one pound of chocolate (454 grams) in this method as a smaller amount is difficult to keep at the proper temperature.

Controlling the Temperature:

Chocolate is harmed by extreme heat and will harden properly only within a narrow temperature span of 88 to 90°F. (31 to 32°C.), and under controlled conditions. Even candy manufacturers, whose procedures are carefully temperature controlled, have problems with chocolate, and they are not always able to avoid the plague of the amateur dipper—the tendency of the cocoa butter to separate from the rest of the ingredients and emerge in gray streaks known in the trade as "bloom." Bloom can affect the best of chocolate coating in hot weather, when the chocolate melts in the daytime and then hardens again in the cool of the evening.

The most important factor in *Professional Chocolate Dipping* is not the easily acquired finger skills but temperature control. Chocolate can be a cranky and demanding substance, particularly sensitive to heat and cold. Ideally, the chocolate should be at exactly 89°F. (31.6°C) for hand-dipping. Mr. Kron says, "You'll just have to accept this." In his classes, however, he does give a reasonable method for testing the temperature of the chocolate, based on normal body temperature of 98.6°F. (37°C.). While cooling, known in the trade as tempering, test the temperature of the coating by dabbing a small amount in the middle of the chin and just below the lower lip. (This is definitely not the time to answer the doorbell.) When the cooled chocolate actually feels cold to the skin, it is of perfect coating consistency. This will be 10 degrees lower than body temperature, or about 89°F. (31.6°C.). It doesn't take too much experience to sense when this temperature has been reached but, failing this test, you can always fall back on the *Easy-Method* of dabbing small amounts on waxed paper: the dab should dry and gloss over in 90 seconds. If the chocolate is not cooled enough, the coating will run off the centers and form heavy bottoms. If the chocolate hardens immediately and is dull rather than glossy, it is too cold. In that case just scrape the coating back into the warm chocolate and remelt.

Weather Conditions and Professional Chocolate Dipping:

You can dip successfully only when you pay careful attention to temperature—of the day and the room as well as of the chocolate. If you are not working in an air-conditioned kitchen, choose a clear cool day when the room temperature is no more than 70°F. (21°C.), free from steam or cooking vapors, and with no direct drafts.

Preparation of Chocolate:

Grate one pound (454 grams) of chocolate by hand. Work as quickly as possible to prevent the chocolate from absorbing moisture from your hands. One pound of grated chocolate will coat approximately sixty ¾-inch centers.

Preparing the Work Area:

The work area should be large enough to hold a tray of centers to be dipped at one end, and a baking sheet lined with waxed paper for receiving the dipped chocolates at the other end. In the middle there must be either a marble slab or formica to use for "working" the chocolate.

Utensils:

1   1-quart double boiler
Wide rubber spatula
Hand grater
Candy thermometer
2   baking sheets lined with waxed paper
Marble slab or formica top

If you have tried the *Easy-Method* chocolate dipping, you will understand something about controlling the temperature of the coating. With all the testing of the temperature of the water used in the double boiler, be extra careful not to let any water drop into the chocolate. Water thickens chocolate, and causes it, in the words of Mr. Kron, to "clunk" together in a solid and unworkable mass.

Step 1: Place the grated chocolate in the top half of the double boiler.

Step 2: Add water to bottom half, but not too much. The top half of the double boiler should not reach the water level below. If this happens the chocolate will burn and cause the dipped candies to be gray streaked.

Step 3: Heat water in bottom half to 140°F. (60°C.) (use a candy thermometer). Turn off heat.

Step 4: Place top half containing the grated chocolate over the bottom half, and stir continuously with rubber spatula, working the chocolate against sides of pan to melt it evenly. When only a few unmelted particles remain, stir rapidly until chocolate is completely melted.

If the water in the bottom of the double boiler cools, replace it with more heated water. Ordinary tap water will probably be warm enough.

Step 5: When the chocolate is fully melted remove from heat, let the hot water in the bottom of the double boiler cool to 110°F. (43°C.). This will take only a few minutes. Keep stirring the chocolate while the water is cooling.

Step 6: Replace top half containing melted chocolate over the bottom half, and stir occasionally to keep solids from settling to the bottom. Never put a lid over melted chocolate. The heat will cause moisture to condense on the underside of the lid and drip down into the chocolate, making it unusable. Keep the melted chocolate over the warm water throughout the dipping process. Replace the warm water, if necessary.

Step 7: With your right hand scoop two handfuls of melted chocolate onto marble slab or formica top and, with the four fingers of the same hand, move the chocolate about with a circular motion, keeping the chocolate in a small pool about 4 inches in diameter. Keep working the chocolate in the circular motion until it reaches 89°F. (32°C.), using body temperature as a guide. It will cool very quickly. Test it by dabbing some on the chin—the most sensitive spot on the human skin. If the chocolate feels cold, it is ready for coating.

Step 8: Position the dipping fingers as for *Easy-Method* hand-dipping. The only difference is that you will be dipping off the marble slab instead of directly from the pan.

Step 9: With your clean left hand—always keep this hand clean and free from chocolate in order to decorate—pick up a center and drop it into the chocolate pool.

Step 10: With the right-hand fingers in the "V" position cover the center thoroughly with chocolate.

Step 11: With the fingers in the same position, scoop up the center, which now has quite a lot of chocolate sticking to it. With the palm up, gently rap the back of your hand on the marble to make the excess chocolate flow back into the pool.

Step 12: The chocolate should remain at coating temperature for about three minutes. When the chocolate becomes too cold and hardens, scoop it up with a spatula and return it to the double boiler to melt again.

Step 13: With the coated center resting in the "V" position of your fingers, turn coated chocolate over onto tray lined with waxed paper at the right side of work area. Be careful not to slide the center around once you have deposited it on the waxed paper. This will wipe the chocolate off the bottom.

Step 14: If center does not drop easily because of stickiness, manipulate it with middle finger-tip to rest against thumb and push it off.

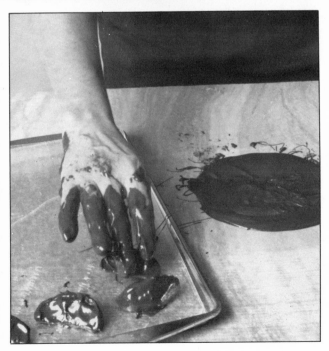

Step 15: After coated center is placed on waxed paper, lift middle finger straight up, pulling string of chocolate to form fancy design. Another method of marking chocolates is to pick up a string of chocolate from the pool with the thumb and first finger, and lay identifying marks across the top. But practice the easy plain string first.

If you find you have been a bit heavy-handed in your first attempt at *Professional* dipping and your chocolates have bare spots and gray streaks, just redip them in the chocolate and recoat them with nuts or other decorations.

How to Make Dipped Chocolate Fruits:

Chocolate-coated fruit is very much in vogue. Either the *Easy-Method* or *Professional* dipping chocolate may be used for this purpose. Have ready an assortment of luscious red strawberries, orange sections, dried apricot halves, pitted dates, and large raisins. Fresh fruit must be free of moisture. Leave at room temperature several hours to dehydrate the dipping surface. Work as quickly as possible and dip either the whole fruit or the tip of the fruit into the melted chocolate. Strawberries and orange sections make a beautiful and tasty combination. One word of warning: Fresh fruits are perishable —dip them the day they are to be eaten.

Chapter 20
CHOCOLATE MOLDING

Whether you are using antique heart molds to give as Valentines or new ones to make delicious chocolate Easter eggs, cleverly molded chocolates will add to the professional-like appearance of any candy assortment.

Molding Small Chocolate Forms Basics:

Properly cooled dipping chocolate may be spooned into small decorative molds to form rectangles, rounds, squares, shells, nuts, or small animals. The tiny individual molds, clever as many of them are, are especially tedious to fill. Professional dippers, who turn out molded chocolates in quantity, use sheet molds. These are sheets of aluminum or plastic with cavities, or indentations, form-ing a wide variety of designs. (See Sources of Supply, p. 218.) You may also improvise and use toy muffin tins or any metal lid with a smooth inside rim.

Easy-Method dipping chocolate is recom-mended for filling chocolate molds because it remains fluid and thin enough for pouring. In the trade a very little lecithin is added to the chocolate to thin the mixture for pouring and molding purposes. Professionals add about 1 teaspoonful (5 ml) to each 3 pounds (1362 grams) of pure chocolate. This ingre-dient is already sparingly present in the summer coating used to custom-blend the *Easy-Method* chocolate coating.

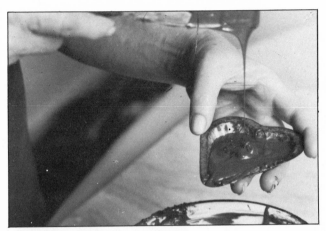

Step 1: Cool the chocolate to dipping consistency. (If you have progressed to this point, it will be easy for you to tell when the chocolate is of the right consistency to spoon into the molds.)

Step 2: Fill the molds, whack the bottoms soundly on a solid surface so the bubbles will rise to the top, and smooth the top surface with a wide spatula to even it off, otherwise it will be difficult to release the chocolate from the molds. Place in the refrigerator until firm.

Step 3: To remove the candies from molds, rap each sharply against a hard surface to loosen the chocolate, then invert over smooth surface. Store in single layers.

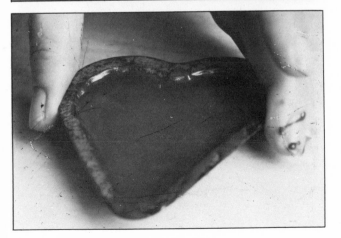

Molding Chocolate Animals, Easter Eggs, and Other Deep Forms:

The professional way of molding Easter eggs, animals and other unusual forms is to use two-piece cast-aluminum molds (truly collector's items), or new plastic molds. (See Sources of Supply, p. 218.) These consist of two halves, hinged together, to mold around the form. They come in a large range of sizes. Start with the smaller molds if you are new at this.

Conditioning the Molds:

Do not wash these molds in soap and water. When using for the first time, brush inside with a little vegetable oil or unsalted butter. Then wipe clean. If using antique molds, wipe and clean with paper towels until all the dark residue of age is removed.

Step 1: First chill the empty molds in the refrigerator. Remove and place the halves on a smooth, level surface. Fill one half to the very top with chocolate of a dipping consistency. With a spatula smooth off any chocolate on the edges that might cause a molding line on the finished form. Close molds together and fasten very well. Shake the form very gently to distribute the chocolate evenly inside the form. The center of the mold will be hollow. When the chocolate seems to have "set" inside the mold, place the form in the refrigerator to harden for several hours or overnight.

Step 2: To remove the form from the mold wear white cotton gloves so the warmth of the fingers will not mar the gloss of the smooth surface and gently tap out form. If the form seems hard to remove, the chocolate has not set sufficiently.

Molding Hollow Shells:

This is the method for molding hollow Easter eggs and making dessert shells.

Step 1: Place the empty chilled mold halves on a smooth, level surface and fill both halves to the top with chocolate of a dipping consistency. Wait for the chocolate to set around the edges. The center should remain melted.

Step 2: Very gently pour the melted center back into the dipping chocolate. With the handle of the spatula gently rap the bottom of the shell, allowing any remaining melted chocolate, to flow from the shell. (It is desirable to have these shells as thin as possible, especially for dessert shells.) Before unmolding, these halves must be cooled in the refrigerator until they have hardened.

Step 3: Unmold the halves by placing on smooth surface and very gently tapping the top of the molds. Again, handle the chocolate with white gloves to keep the warmth of the fingers from marring the smooth surface.

Fill the dessert shells with fruit or ice cream.

Chocolate Leaves and Chocolate Lace

Both of these are used to decorate elegant continental-type cakes and other rich desserts. You can make your own from left-over dipping chocolate and store in airtight containers.

How to Make Chocolate Leaves:

Select desired number of fresh rose leaves. Wash and dry.

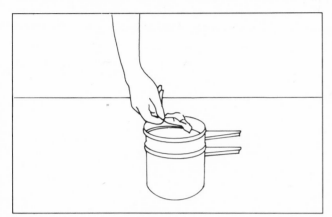

Step 1: Pull a single rose leaf, upside down, over the surface of a pot of dipping chocolate or paint the chocolate on the leaf with a pastry brush.

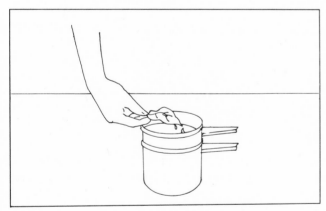

Step 2: Remove any extra chocolate by tapping leaf against the side of the pan. Then place leaf, chocolate side up, on a baking sheet lined with waxed paper and place in refrigerator to harden.

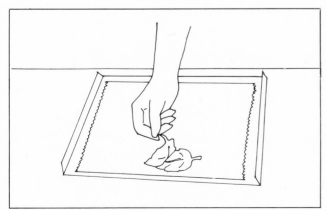

Step 3: When the chocolate has hardened, just peel off the leaf. You'll have perfect chocolate leaves with the veins from the real leaf imprinted in the chocolate.

How to Make Chocolate Lace:

This requires a pastry decorating bag and small writing tube tip.

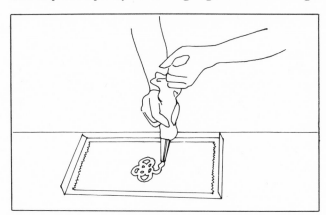

Step 1: Fill the pastry decorating bag with chocolate of a dipping consistency. Take the end of the pastry bag in two fingers as with a pencil and squeeze the chocolate onto a baking sheet lined with waxed paper, creating your own designs. Place in the refrigerator to harden.

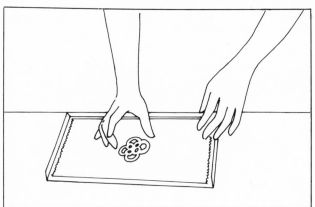

Step 2: Lift the chocolate lace from the waxed paper. Your hands should be cool while doing this or the chocolate will melt. Rubbing hands with ice cubes and then drying them thoroughly will cool them sufficiently for handling the hardened lace.

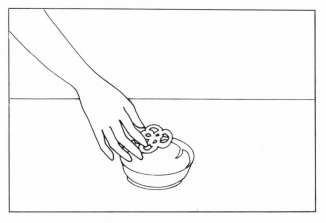

Step 3: Place the chocolate lace onto the dessert to be garnished.

Special Instructions for Coating Large Forms:

With the use of luscious Chocolate, Bonbon, Caramel, or Summer Coating, there is nothing more delicious than homemade party motifs. These instructions are written for the novice; the professional candymaker will already know how to coat large forms.

It is preferable to have forms that are smallish as they will be easier to handle in the dipping mixture, and also because the larger ones are too rich to eat.

All forms to be dipped should be at room temperature and turned frequently to crust and glaze on all sides. This helps stabilize the surface for dipping.

Recommended Centers for Large Forms:
Refer to listing in each section for Chocolate, Bonbon, Caramel, or Summer Coating. I especially like the pastel variations of *White Fudge* for Easter-egg centers because the delicate shades and fruit flavors are just right for the season.

Dipping Large Forms:

For dipping larger confections of this type, you will need plenty of coating in your pan, and, of course, it must be at the correct dipping temperature. Two pounds (909 grams) of coating should cover about four pounds (1818 grams), depending upon the form to be dipped.

Step 1: Pierce with skewers the ends of the forms to be dipped. I recommend the small size skewer used to truss poultry. The thinness of the skewer will leave a scarcely noticeable hole, which can be touched up later with extra coating or decorating frosting.

Step 2: Using the skewers as handles, dip each form into the coating, rolling it around to thoroughly coat the surface. Shake well to drain excess coating back into the pan.

Step 3: Still using the skewers as handles, rest the form in a horizontal position between two piles of books, or other suitable objects, so that the form will dry without marring the finish of the coating. Leave in this position for decorating.

Step 4: Remove the skewers and touch up the holes with frosting.

Chapter 21
SUMMER COATING FOR CONFECTIONS

Summer Coating is also sold as white coating, the same ingredient I use in the *Easy-Method* chocolate dipping. (See Sources of Supply, p. 218.)

Candies made with this non-chocolate, low-cholesterol coating are especially desirable in summer because its melting point is higher and the temperature control not nearly so delicate as that of chocolate. Summer Coating is grated by hand and melted in the top part of the double boiler over simmering, but not boiling, water as in the preparation of the ingredients for *Easy-Method* chocolate dipping. Because of its higher melting point of about 100°F. (38°C), you will have none of the hot and humid weather worries of the chocolate dipper. In comparison, the summer-coating of candies is casual in the extreme, especially easy for the amateur.

If you find yourself, as I did, with a quantity of white summer coating left over from custom-blending dipping chocolate, it can be left white, or tinted and flavored to add a variety of centers to your candy-box assortment. Use oil-base food colors such as coloring pastes, and flavoring oils are recommended instead of extracts. See Coloring and Flavoring Charts, pp. 30-31. With the lovely pastel colors of cream, yellow, pink, green, and butterscotch, your candy boxes will look like miniature summer gardens. A little cocoa or carob powder may be mixed with the summer coating to give it a light-brown color.

Recommended Centers:

Any center suitable for dipping in chocolate can be dipped in Summer Coating. A combination of coated marshmallows and jelly candies with their cool frosted summer look is very attractive and suitable for the person on a low-cholesterol diet. Children like Summer Coating on pretzels, cereals, dried fruits, cookie wafers, nuts, or any other inspiration of the moment.

Preparing the Ingredients:

Summer Coating melts faster when grated by hand. *Caution:* You may use an electric food processor, but do not attempt to grate in the blender. The coating tends to clog the blender blades. Hand-grate the Summer Coating, but no less than ½ pound (227 grams) or 2 cups (480 ml). This amount will coat approximately thirty dozen ¾-inch centers.

Preparing the Work Area:

See photographs for *Easy-Method Chocolate Dipping,* pp. 147-156.

Utensils:

1   1-quart double boiler
Wide rubber spatula
2   cup measure
Hand grater
Candy thermometer
2   baking sheets lined with waxed paper

Blending Summer Coating Mixture:

Put grated coating in top half of double boiler; put water in lower half. Do not let top half actually touch water. Bring water *almost* to boil, then stir coating continuously with a wide rubber spatula until melted. Remove pan of coating from over the hot water. Place candy thermometer in hot water and cool it to about 140°F. (60°C.). Continue to stir coating until the mixture has cooled to lukewarm, about 100°F. (38°C). Add coloring and flavoring. Be careful not to let any moisture fall into coating, which will be somewhat thicker than chocolate. As in chocolate dipping, a string of coating about 1½ inches long will dangle from the end of the rubber spatula. If the coating is too cold, and you have waited too long to dip, the coating will harden on the fingers. In this case, pass these first candies out as kitchen samples and reheat the coating over the hot water in the bottom of the double boiler, which may be kept over very low heat. *Caution:* At no time during the melting process let the water come to a boil. If it does, the mixture will not melt uniformly, but will first begin to melt, then crumble, and become impossible to handle. If the coating seems too thin, and you have heavy bottoms on your centers, the mixture is not cool enough. The centers will then have to be redipped for a heavier coating.

Leave the rubber spatula in the pan, and place the melted coating in the middle of the prepared work area. Stir the mixture occasionally during the dipping process.

Hand-Dipping:

Review photographs in Steps 1 through 9 for hand-dipping as in *Easy-Method Chocolate Dipping,* pp. 147-156. If you hand-dip, or use a dipping fork, dip directly from the pan of melted coating.

Step 1: With palm facing you, hold up the middle and index fingers of your right hand in a "V" for victory sign.

Step 2: Enclose your thumb and the rest of your fingers. The two extended fingers form the "V" for your dipping fork.

Step 3: Throughout the dipping process the left hand must be kept clean and free from chocolate in order to decorate the chocolates with nuts, sprinkles, etc. With the clean left hand, drop a center from the tray on the left side of your work area into the Summer Coating.

Step 4: Place the right hand formed in the "V" dipping position into the chocolate mixture and roll the center over to coat.

Step 5: With the fingers in the "V" position, the hand palm side up, scoop up the center, which will have quite a lot of the melted coating sticking to it.

Step 6: With the coated center resting in the fork of the middle and index fingers, gently rap the back of your fingers on the edge of the pan to make the excess coating flow back into the pan.

Step 7: With the coated center still resting in the "V" position of your fingers, turn the confection over onto tray lined with waxed paper on your right side of work area. Do not slide the coated center around once you have deposited it on the waxed paper.

Step 8: If center does not drop easily because of stickiness, manipulate it with middle fingertip to rest against thumb and push it off.

Step 9: After coated center is placed on waxed paper, lift middle finger straight up, pulling string of coating to form fancy design.

Reheating Dipping Mixture:

The mixture should remain at dipping temperature for 15 to 20 minutes. If the mixture cools and becomes too thick, remelt the coating over warm water. *Caution:* Take care the temperature of the melted coating does not rise above 110°F. (43°C.).

Decorating Coated Centers:

This must be done as soon as possible after the centers have been dipped. A helper is needed if the candies are to be decorated with a pastry tube.

How to Use Leftover Summer Coating:

White Almond Bark Candy: Combine 2 cups (480 ml) melted summer coating (tinted if desired) with 2 cups (480 ml) lightly roasted slivered almonds. Using a wide spatula spread on clean baking sheet to a depth of about ¼ inch and cool until firm. Break into eating-size pieces. To look more like bark, the coating may be scored with the tines of a fork before it has set. Crushed peppermint-stick candy may be substituted for the almonds. This popular candy can be made for less than half the price of the bought confection, so it is an economical everyday sweet for the neighborhood crowd.

Macaroon Creams: These are candy cookies and require no baking. Be prepared for them to disappear very fast. Melt 2 cups (480 ml) hand-grated summer coating. Add 2 tablespoons (30 ml) light cream or milk, 1½ cups (360 ml) flaked coconut and ¼ teaspoon (1.25 ml) almond extract. Stir with spatula until well mixed. Drop mixture from a teaspoon onto waxed paper. Cool until firm.

Yield: About twenty-four cookies.

Caring for Finished Candies with Summer Coating:

Although these candies seem to harden very quickly and have a nice sheen, they should be permitted to stand for an hour or two at room temperature to dry completely before

being removed from the waxed paper. Store
as for chocolates in single layers in airtight
containers in a cool, dry place; never in direct
sunlight. Candies with Summer Coating,
because of their high tolerance to warm
temperatures and humidity, can be packaged
and mailed as gifts throughout the year.

Molding Summer Coating:

Refer to Chapter 20.

Chapter 22
BONBON-COATED CANDIES

Fondant is the basis of all bonbons. The word "fondant" comes from the French language and means "cream-like."

The only ingredients needed for making fondant are granulated sugar, water, and some inverting substance such as corn syrup and/or cream of tartar. "Inverting" in sugar cookery reverses the graininess of a boiled sugar and water mixture. I add both corn syrup and cream of tartar because it is necessary to have a very creamy fondant to make these candies.

Just as soon as the fondant has been cooled and worked with a spatula until it is smooth and creamy, the mass is divided into two portions and stored in the refrigerator for two days. One portion is then remelted in the top part of a double boiler to be used as coating. The other portion is used to form the centers to be dipped in the melted mixture.

Bonbon dipping is not expensive, but it is tedious, and you must be familiar with the technique of crystallizing sugar. One single undissolved crystal, or the least amount of stirring while cooking, will cause the mixture to be hard and grainy. Because of the high temperature of the bonbon coating, you'll need to learn how to use a dipping fork to remove the dipped centers from the pan. You must also keep the dipping mixture just warm enough and fluid enough to coat the centers and to form the string, or crown, the mark of the true French bonbon. However, patience and practice will reward you with extremely attractive candies.

Basic Fondant

(Recommended as Centers for Chocolate or Summer Coating)

Fondant must be made and ripened at least two days before bonbons are to be dipped. Choose a clear, cool day for making the fondant to use for bonbons and for coating the centers. Humid weather will cause the confections to be sticky.

Utensils:

1   4-quart heavy saucepan
1   wooden spoon
2   cup measure
1   set of measuring spoons
Candy thermometer
1   metal or wooden spatula, 3-5 inches wide
1   large baking sheet with sides

Ingredients:

4   cups (960 ml) granulated sugar, sifted
1½ cups (360 ml) water
¼   cup (60 ml) light corn syrup
¼   teaspoon (1.25 ml) cream of tartar
Dash of salt

Preparation:

1. Put the sugar, water, corn syrup, cream of tartar, and salt in saucepan. Cook over low heat, stirring constantly with the wooden spoon, until sugar is dissolved. *Caution:* Do not let mixture come to a boil. You should not be able to feel sugar grains when you rub the spoon against the sides of the saucepan.

2. Remove from heat and, with a damp towel or small sponge, wipe any remaining grains from the sides of the pan above the liquid level.

3. Return the mixture to moderate heat.

4. Cover the pan long enough for the mixture to boil, which should take 2 or 3 minutes—no more!

5. Uncover the pan and *again* wipe down the sides to remove sugar grains.

6. Insert the candy thermometer.

7. Cook slowly, without stirring, until the thermometer registers 238°F. (114°C.) or until a small quantity dropped into cold water forms a soft ball (p. 26).

8. Remove from heat.

9. Rinse baking sheet with cold water and gently pour the mixture over the damp surface. Do not scrape pan!

10. Cool to lukewarm (110°F. or 43°C.). The syrup should feel just warm, not hot.

11. Work fondant with spatula by lifting and folding edges of candy mass toward the center.

12. When the candy loses its translucency and begins to become opaque and creamy, gather into a ball and knead with lightly buttered hands until the mass is smooth and creamy. Knead only enough to make it hold together.

13. Divide the fondant and form in two round balls. One half will be used to make approximately sixty centers and the remaining half will be remelted to form the coating for the centers.

14. Wrap each ball in waxed paper and store in airtight container in the refrigerator to ripen for at least 48 hours but not more than 10 days.

After 10 days the fondant will be too soft to form centers for dipping in the coating. If this should happen, *Quick Buttercreme*

Fondant may be used to form the centers. Remelt all the soft fondant for dipping purposes.

Flavoring and Coloring Bonbons:

Bonbons should be delicately tinted and flavored to match their centers. See Coloring and Flavoring Charts, pp. 30-31. Just remember to use a very light touch when adding color. There is no going back if you added too much.

The classic French bonbon center is flavored with peppermint, rum, cherry, or vanilla. Flatten the ball to be used for the centers and add ½ teaspoon (2.5 ml) of any of the above flavorings or other flavoring to taste. Knead with hands until well blended.

Fresh fruit, mint leaves, and flower petals may also be dipped in Bonbon Coating.

Bonbon Fondant as Coating

Prepare the work area as for *Easy-Method Chocolate Dipping*, pp. 147-156.

Utensils:

1   1-quart double boiler
1   wooden spoon
1   dipping fork
1   set measuring spoons
Candy thermometer (optional)
2   baking sheets lined with waxed paper

Preparation:

1. Put reserved half of fondant in top half of double boiler; put water in lower half. Do not let top half actually touch water.

2. Heat fondant over simmering, but not boiling, water.

3. Stir gently with wooden spoon until mixture has melted.

4. Add ½ teaspoon (2.5 ml) flavoring and coloring. Continue stirring until mixture is hot and thin. A crust will begin to appear as soon as the stirring stops, therefore work steadily to dip fondant centers. During dipping, keep stirring melted fondant to remove crust.

5. Remove the fondant, still over the hot water, to the middle of the work area.

6. Wrap foil around the middle of the double boiler to seal in the heat of the hot water.

Bonbon Dipping Fork Basics:

Step 1: With the clean left hand drop a center into melted fondant and push below surface with dipping fork.

Step 2: Pick up the center with the loop on the end of the dipping fork and shake very gently to drain coating back into the pan.

Step 3: Carefully draw the coated center on the dipping fork across the edge of the pan to remove any excess melted fondant, being careful not to scrape too much fondant from bonbon.

Step 4: Turn the dipping fork over to place the coated bonbon onto waxed-paper-lined baking sheet at right side of working area. Hold dipping fork in contact with coated bonbon for a few seconds, then lift it off, pulling up a string of coating to make the traditional swirled crown. If, when you lift the fork, the crown is ragged and broken, you have waited too long before removing the loop of the dipping fork. If the crown melts back down into the bonbon, you took the fork away too soon. A little practice will improve your technique.

If the mixture becomes too thick for dipping, add 1 teaspoon (5 ml) of hot water at a time to thin the coating.

If you are using a homemade dipping fork, you will not be able to form the string on the crown. Just sprinkle bonbons with chocolate or multi-colored sprinkles.

Caring for Finished Bonbons:

Let dipped bonbons stand at least one hour to harden and then turn them over carefully on their sides so that bottoms may dry.

Bonbon Coating does not contain fat, so the candies will not keep for any length of time. One week is about the limit. Store them in an airtight container at room temperature. In a refrigerator, they will harden and the coating will crack from the cold.

How to Use Leftover Bonbon Coating to Make Party Mints:

To make dropped patties even in size and perfectly round, you need a smooth, level surface. Waxed paper or a lightly oiled baking sheet serves very well, but I like my sister's suggestion: "Wash and thoroughly dry the underneath side of a rubberized dish-drainer mat." Lightly oiled, the ridges of the mat give that professional finish to the patties. Confectioners' supply houses carry special vinyl mats that produce the same result.

The actual dropping can be done two ways: from the tip of a teaspoon or through a funnel. The funnel has a wooden stopper that helps gauge the correct amount of melted fondant for each mint. You can purchase such a funnel from a confectioners' supply house, or you can make your own simply by cutting off the bottom half of a narrow-necked plastic bottle and using the handle

end of a wooden spoon as a stopper to control the flow of the melted bonbon coating through the neck of the bottle.

How to Use Funnel and Stopper to Drop Mint Patties:

Step 1: Fill the funnel with stopper in place over a wide-mouth jar.

Step 2: Pour the warm bonbon coating into the funnel and remove from over jar.

Step 3: Hold the funnel by the handle and, with your free hand, pull up the wooden stopper to release the coating to form a small mint no larger than a quarter. Continue until all mints have been formed.

If the bonbon coating is at the proper temperature, the mints will be smooth on top. If it is beginning to cool and harden, slight peaks will form as you drop the patties. To prevent this, remelt the coating over hot water.

Step 4: As soon as the mints are firm, loosen and lift them. If they stand too long, they will break when you take them up.

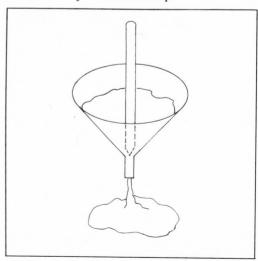

Chapter 23
CARAMEL-COATED CONFECTIONS

If you have caramel freaks on your gift-giving list—as I do—you will want to include a few of these luscious morsels in your candy-box assortments. The dipping is not as fussy as in coating bonbons because the temperature control is not as exacting. Any center firm enough to withstand the 140-150°F. (60-66°C.) dipping temperature of the liquid caramel may be used. Because of the high temperature of the caramel, you'll need to use the dipping fork to remove the centers from the pan.

Recommended Centers:

(See index for recipes.)

Uncooked Fondant
Marzipan
Fudge
Nougat
Brittle
Toffee
Butter Crunch
Dried Fruits
Nuts
Commercial Marshmallows

Not Recommended:

Creamy Cooked Fondant
Soft Divinity
Handmade Marshmallows
Jellies

Caramel-coated confections are usually rolled in chopped nuts or coconut. This may be done alone, but a kitchen helper is truly a help. One person may dip, and the other roll the coated pieces while the caramel is still warm. This recipe will coat approximately 24 centers.

Once the caramel-coated candies have cooled to room temperature they may be redipped in Chocolate Coating. This is often done in making candy bars and Easter eggs.

Caramel Coating

The Caramel Coating will take about 2½ hours to cook because it requires frequent raising and lowering of the temperature of the cooking syrup. This high-low (slacking back) cooking process produces a particularly soft and butter-rich coating. You can prepare the syrup ahead of time and reheat for dipping.

This recipe was developed especially for coating candies and other confections. It

will be too soft to be poured in a pan to be cut in eating-size squares.

Utensils:

1   1-quart heavy saucepan
1   wooden spoon
1   dipping fork
1   set measuring spoons
1   set measuring cups
Candy thermometer
2   baking sheets (Do not line these with waxed paper because the caramel will stick to the surface.)

Ingredients:

1   cup (240 ml) granulated sugar, sifted
⅔   cup (160 ml) light corn syrup
¼   teaspoon (1.25 ml) salt
¼   cup (60 ml) butter (½ stick)
1½ cups (360 ml) whole milk
½   teaspoon (2.5 ml) vanilla

Preparation:

1. Put the sugar, corn syrup, and salt in saucepan. Cook over low heat, stirring constantly with the wooden spoon, until sugar is dissolved. *Caution:* Do not let mixture come to a boil. You should not be able to feel sugar grains when you rub the spoon against the sides of the saucepan.

2. Cook slowly, without stirring, until a small quantity dropped into cold water forms a firm ball (248°F. or 120°C.). (This first cooking will ordinarily take no longer than 5 minutes.)

3. Add butter and stir with wooden spoon until melted. Then stir continuously while adding ½ cup (120 ml) milk and cook again to 248°F. or 120°C.

4. Stir in another ½ cup (120 ml) milk and recook to 248°F. or 120°C.

5. Add the last ½ cup (120 ml) milk and stir continuously over moderate heat until a small quantity dropped into cold water forms a soft ball (240°F. or 116°C.). During the final cooking do not panic if the mixture seems to be browning on the bottom of the pan. This is the normal caramelizing of the syrup, which gives the candies their delicious flavor.

6. Remove the mixture from the heat and cool down to about 145°F. or 63°C.

7. Stir in vanilla.

Yield: 2 cups (480 ml).

Caramel Dipping Fork Basics:

While the coating is cooling prepare the work area as for *Easy Method Chocolate Dipping* (pp. 147-156)—with one exception. The coating must be kept warm enough to be workable during the dipping of the centers. You can place the pan of warm coating on an electric hot tray or other heating unit. The alternative is to return the mixture to the stove for reheating as needed.

Step 1: With the clean left hand drop a center into the pan of melted caramel and push below surface with dipping fork.

Step 2: Pick up the center with the loop on the end of the dipping fork and shake to drain excess coating back into the pan.

Step 3: Carefully draw the coated center on the dipping fork across the edge of the pan to remove all excess coating.

Step 4: Turn the dipping fork over to deposit the coated caramel onto lightly greased baking sheet to your right on the working area.

Step 5: Roll the coated caramels in ground nuts, coconut, et cetera, while they are still

warm and place on lightly greased baking sheet to cool.

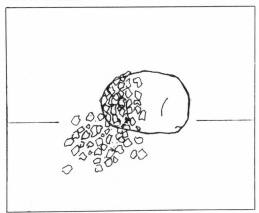

How to Use Leftover Caramel Coating:

You may well build your candy-making reputation by recreating the famous "turtles" with leftover caramel and dipping chocolate. Twelve turtles will weigh approximately 1 pound (454 grams).

Turtles: (See photographs on following page.) Spread pecan halves on baking sheet to a depth of ½ inch. The amount of pecans

needed will depend on the amount of dipping caramel left over. With a teaspoon drop melted Caramel Coating onto pecan halves. Do not make these drops larger than 1 inch in diameter or place drops too close together. When the caramel has cooled and set, lift out the turtle centers and place them on cooling rack until firm. The remainder of the pecans may be used another time. Melt and spoon leftover dipping chocolate over the caramel on cooling rack. Let stand until chocolate has hardened.

Caring for Finished Caramel-Coated Candies:

Although these candies are edible as soon as they harden, their flavor is improved if permitted to stand for 24 hours. Store as for chocolates in airtight containers in a cool, dry place. Caramel-coated candies have long-keeping qualities because of their high butterfat content.

Step 1

Step 2

Step 3

Step 4

Chapter 24
GLAZED AND CANDIED FRUITS AND NUTS

What is the sorcery that transforms fruits and nuts from only visions of sugarplums into delicious realities? The secret lies in a thin, crackly, clear glaze called glacé syrup for fresh fruits and a heavier granulated coating for dried fruits, citrus peels, and nuts. Brighten your festive table with an edible centerpiece, using a combination of any of the four.

Corn syrup is in the recipe for glazing syrup to retard crystallization. Be careful to remove sugar grains before the first boil. An ambitious stray grain of sugar can make the syrup over-crystallized, and give you candied fruits instead of a clear fruit glaze.

Preparation of Fruits:

Step 1: Use only fresh fruits that are in prime and firm condition with no surface blemishes or breaks that will leak moisture.

Step 2: Work with glazing syrup on a coolish, dry day with the barometric pressure normal and steady.

Step 3: Glazed fresh fruits lose their magic within a matter of hours. If you are coating a large quantity, divide the fruits into several batches for successive dipping. All fruit must be at room temperature and have a dry surface. Orange and tangerine sections must be dried on racks for at least six hours, or place them in a warm, turned-off oven for approximately 2 to 3 minutes.

Recommended Fruits:

Fresh Strawberries
Oranges
Tangerines
Dried Fruits
Cherries
Grapes
Small Plums

Dipping Fresh Fruits:

Strawberries and cherries may be dipped by their stems. For other fruits you will need to use a dipping fork. This may also be done at the table in your fondue pot, using the forks for individual spearing. Have small bowls of ice water handy. After the fruit is dipped it will be very hot for a few seconds. For rapid cooling plunge the hot fruit in the ice water before placing on the serving plate.

Dipping Glaze

Utensils:

1   1-quart double boiler
1   wooden spoon
1   set measuring cups
Candy thermometer
2   baking sheets lined with waxed paper or lightly oiled

Ingredients:

2   cups (480 ml) granulated sugar, sifted
1   cup (240 ml) water
⅓   cup (80 ml) light corn syrup

Preparation:

1. Lightly grease the sides of the top part of the double boiler.

2. Add the sugar, water, and corn syrup. Cook directly over low heat, stirring constantly with the wooden spoon, until sugar is dissolved. *Caution:* Do not let mixture come to a boil. You should not be able to feel sugar grains when you rub the spoon against the sides of the pan.

3. Remove from heat and, with a damp paper towel or small sponge, wipe any remaining grains from the sides of the pan above the liquid level.

4. Return the mixture to moderate heat.

5. Cover the pan long enough for the mixture to boil, 2 or 3 minutes—no more!

6. Uncover pan and *again* wipe down the sides to remove sugar grains.

7. Clip on the candy thermometer.

8. Cook slowly, without stirring, until the thermometer registers 290°F. or 143°C. (syrup forms a soft crack (p. 26) in cold water).

9. Remove from heat and place top part of double boiler over lower half containing hot, not boiling, water.

10. Dip each moisture-free fruit, holding it by stem or using dipping fork.

11. Place fruits on waxed paper or lightly oiled baking sheet to dry.

Yield: This amount of syrup will coat about 2 pounds (909 grams) of fruit.

Variations:

Candied Grapefruit and Orange Peels: These have longer keeping qualities than glazed fresh fruits. Simmer the peels in the syrup until tender to help preserve and keep them moist. These will keep almost indefinitely, which makes them particularly good as gifts for mailing.

Candied Flowers, Petals, and Leaves: Small flowers, petals, and leaves, firm and glittering with crystallization, are among the most elegant of all possible candy. They are often used as decorations. Lovely on cakes and Easter eggs, enchanting twinkling among chocolates and other candies.

Ideally you should pick the flowers and leaves early in the morning while they are at their peak of freshness. Violets, rose petals, and mint leaves are most suitable for crystallizing.

Chocolate-Coated Grapefruit and Orange Peels

For this procedure roll the candied peels in confectioners' sugar and shake off excess before dipping in Chocolate Coating. See Easy-Method Chocolate-Dipping instructions (pp. 147-156). *These are highly recommended for quantity gift giving.*

Ruby-red grapefruit makes the most beautiful color of candied peel, but add yellow for contrast. If the peel you use turns out to be the thick kind, scrape away some of the inner white pith but not every bit of it. This is what soaks up the syrup mixture and keeps the peel tender longer.

Preparation:

1. Cut grapefruit or orange peel into ¼-inch strips.

2. Cover with cold water in saucepan. Bring to slow boil, then drain.

3. Repeat this process two more times. The final time cook slowly until peel is tender.

4. Test by piercing one of the strips with the tip of a sharp knife.

5. Drain well and let dry on rack.

Preparing the Syrup:

Use the recipe for *Dipping Glaze* (p. 188) but omit the corn syrup.

1. Cook syrup slowly, without stirring, until the thermometer registers 238°F. or 114°C. (syrup forms a soft ball (p. 26) in cold water).

2. Keep heat low and add peels from 3 or 4 oranges or about 3 grapefruit halves. Do not crowd these too much. Continue to cook slowly until peel begins to look transparent and has absorbed almost all the syrup.

3. Lift peel out of pan with slotted spoon and place on waxed paper in single layer with a little space between each strip.

4. Cool to lukewarm but, while still sticky, drop peels, a few strips at a time, into a small bowl of granulated sugar. Roll them around to coat each strip.

5. Place on waxed paper to dry. Sometimes it is necessary to coat these strips twice.

Candied Nuts

Glazed and sugared nuts are traditionally associated with formal dinners, weddings, teas, and winter holiday festivities. Preparing them is truly the work of a sophisticated cook.

Because these confections have much longer keeping qualities than most confections, you can make them long in advance and hold them in reserve for that important event or gift. They will keep for many weeks if refrigerated or frozen in airtight containers.

Coating nuts is very easy. There is nothing to fret about if your cooked syrup turns slightly grainy—it just gives a more crystallized texture to the coated nuts. If you have the problem of under-cooked syrup, roll the sticky nuts in additional granulated sugar. No one will be the wiser.

Preparing the Syrup:

Use the recipe for *Dipping Glaze* (p. 188.)

1. Cook slowly, without stirring, until the thermometer registers 235°F. or 113°C. (syrup forms a soft ball (p. 26) in cold water).

2. Remove from heat and add ½ teaspoon (2.5 ml) flavoring oil or 2 teaspoons (10 ml) flavoring extract. One tablespoon (15 ml) brandy, bourbon, or rum may be substituted for the oil or extract.

3. Stir 1½ pounds (682 grams) of nuts (any kind) into the cooked syrup with a wooden spoon and continue stirring until mixture is thick and the nuts are thoroughly coated.

4. Turn mass onto lightly oiled baking sheet and, using two forks, separate the nuts into clusters or individual nut halves.

5. Let the nuts cool to room temperature and store in airtight containers in refrigerator or freezer. Will keep indefinitely.

Yield: About 2 pounds (909 grams.)

Spiced Nuts

These highly flavored marshmallow-coated nuts are very colorful and have long-keeping qualities.

Preparation:

1. Prepare *Dipping Glaze* (p. 188) in 2-quart heavy saucepan over direct heat.

2. Cook slowly, without stirring, until thermometer registers 238°F. or 114°C. (syrup forms a soft ball (p. 26) in cold water).

3. Remove from heat and with wooden spoon blend in 20 large marshmallows or about 2 cups (480 ml); add ¼ teaspoon (1.25 ml) oil of cinnamon and a few drops of red food coloring. Continue stirring until well mixed.

4. Add 6 cups (1440 ml) walnut or pecan halves and gently stir until well coated. Try to keep nuts separated as much as possible by continuous stirring during the coating process.

5. Turn out onto lightly oiled baking sheet and continue to separate halves, using two forks.

6. Cool to room temperature and store in airtight container. Will keep indefinitely.

Yield: 2½ pounds (1,136 grams).

Frosted Fresh Fruits

This is the standard at-home process used by the Victorians for coating petals and leaves.

Preparation:

1. Lightly beat 1 egg white with 2 tablespoons (30 ml) water in small bowl.

2. Put 1 cup (240 ml) sifted granulated sugar in another small bowl.

3. Hold flower, petal, or leaf with tweezers and dip in the egg-white mixture, shaking off the excess. Then dip into bowl of sugar. If the object is not thoroughly coated, the process may be repeated.

4. Place on baking sheet lined with brown wrapping paper and let stand in slow oven (170°F. or 77°C.) until dry.

5. Remove from oven and cool to room temperature.

6. Store in airtight container in cool, dry place.

Variations:

Clusters of grapes, strawberries, cherries, or other small whole fruits may be hand-dipped in the above egg-white mixture and then placed on waxed paper. Sprinkle granulated sugar over the freshly dipped fruit, turning it until all sides are thoroughly coated. Leave on waxed paper to dry. This should coat 6 to 8 servings of frosted fruit.

THE CANDY STORE

Now the time has come to create your own candy store with delicious confections and innovative packaging.

In this section: all the directions you'll need for decorating candies and Easter eggs, creative wrapping, storing, freezing, boxing, and mailing, plus a Candy Calendar for gift giving. You'll find complete instructions for covering recycled containers, making your own gift paper, and forming individual crinkle cups from kitchen foil.

Welcome to my Candy Store!

Decorating Confections

Easter eggs, dropped fondant mints, and bonbons are the traditionally decorated confections. A chocolatier would consider it almost a sacrilege to over-embellish any other expensive handmade candy.

Take this author's word, the most expensive-looking handmade candies can be decorated to equal those of a professional candymaker by using already prepared tubes of frosting from the supermarket in pastels such as pink, green, and yellow.

Candy decorating with supermarket frosting tubes—and this is what the professionals use—depends mainly upon proper hand pressure and holding the tube at a 45° angle.

Remember, always massage the tubes at room temperature to redistribute the coloring before using. Never store tubes in the refrigerator or freezer and attempt to decorate before the contents have reached room temperature. If necessary, place tubes in lukewarm water first. Apply designs freehand onto candies. Keep designs simple and preferably pastel.

Use the flat surface of a baking sheet for practice. If your first efforts are less than perfect (and they will be) just scrape and squeeze again.

How to Use Frosting Tubes to Make Simple Designs:

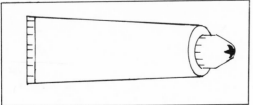

Fine lines, scrolls, stems, and dots: Use the writing tip and hold it at a 45° angle as you would a pen to write on any other surface.

Examples:

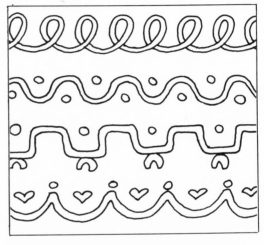

Leaves, flower petals, and border scrolls: Use the leaf tip and hold it at a 45° angle. For a fat leaf use more pressure than for a longer flower petal. Give a slight twist to the tube to release the frosting from the leaf or petal. Link leaves or petals together to make border scrolls.

Examples:

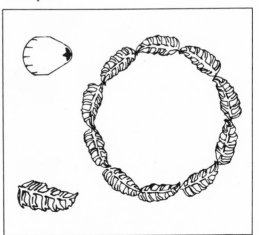

Star flowers and shell border designs: Use the star tip and hold it straight; do not angle the tube; apply enough pressure to form star design. Lift up and twist slightly to release the frosting from the star flower. Hold the tube at a 45° angle and form desired border by intermittently increasing and decreasing the pressure.

Examples:

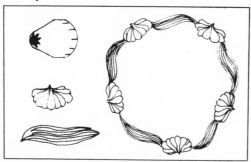

Roses: Use a petal tip and flower nail. To form a rosebud fasten a 1½-inch square of waxed paper on the flower nail with a dot of frosting. Then form a small mound of frosting on the center of the paper. Hold the nail with the thumb and forefinger of your left hand. Next, rest the wide end of the tip on the nail, then squeeze, making two tight turns for a rosebud. Then squeeze the tube and turn the nail to make individual rose petals. After the first petal is made, stop the pressure and make second petal slightly overlapping the first. Continue until the desired size of the rose is complete. Let dry and attach to candy confection with dot of frosting.

Examples:

How to Decorate Easter Eggs:

For the beginner it is preferable to have an egg that is solid, that is, one that has a cream center and has been dipped in coating.

Let coated eggs dry for about four hours before decorating. Pierce the end of each egg with a thin metal or wooden skewer and suspend the egg between two piles of heavy books. This will give you more working surface and the egg can be rotated for easy decorating. Decorate with the traditional scrolls, flowers, and "Easter Greetings." It is customary to pipe individual names on eggs for parties and Easter-morning hunts.

Examples:

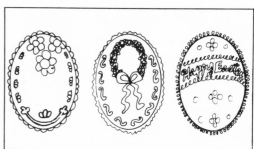

How to Decorate Bonbons and Mints:

The traditional decoration on a white fondant-coated bonbon is a single silver dragee not larger than ⅛ inch in diameter. But this French sweetmeat may also be decorated with flowers and frills. Plan to serve decorated candies within a few days because the frosting has a tendency to become too hard and brittle to be palatable.

After-dinner mints can be conversation treats to hail any occasion and charm the guests! Use fondant or hand-dipped mints.

The following are a few decorative suggestions. I like to decorate white bonbons or mints with a little red dot for a holly berry and a green leaf for Christmastime and use the pastel colors for Easter, Mother's Day, and other appropriate occasions.

Examples:

Candy Calendar For Gift Giving

The sweetest custom of any holiday can be a gift of candy from your own kitchen. Making an assortment of luscious morsels to give as presents to family and friends speaks louder than words. Knowing their likes and dislikes is the ultimate of thoughtfulness in the art of giving. Since trusting to memory is tricky business, it is sensible to use a card-file system to record personal preferences, birthdays, anniversaries, and other important dates.

Remember, however, giving is an act of love. It needs neither occasion nor a special holiday; in fact, the element of surprise makes an unexpected gift of beautifully wrapped candies doubly appreciated.

Chocolate Greeting Cards:

So very easy to do! Wrapped in foil and then carefully packaged, these can be sent via the U.S. mail.

Let your chocolate-dipping expertise take over for all occasions. Birthdays, Mother's Day, or even "get well" messages are but a few of the personal greetings that can be expressed on a block of molded chocolate. All you need are frosting tubes with which to decorate and write your special wish. Summer Coating, too, can be used to create a fantasy in pastels.

First, read through the instructions for molding chocolate forms (pp. 165-171) and decorating confections (pp. 195-197).

Greeting cards can be molded any size and shape. I use the lid of a metal box, measuring 6¾ inches by 4¼ inches and ⅝ inch deep. This size holds exactly one-half pound of dipping chocolate.

Materials:

2 cups (480 ml) custom-blended grated
  chocolate
1 molding tin
Frosting tubes with writing, star, flower, and
  leaf tips

Step 1: Prepare the dipping chocolate
according to the instructions in Chapter
18, (pp. 147&156).

Step 2: Pour the melted chocolate into the
molding tin.

Step 3: Rap the tin smartly on a hard
surface to make the bubbles rise to the
surface, which will give the bottom a smooth
surface for decorating.

Step 4: Place the mold in the refrigerator to
harden the chocolate.

Step 5: Remove and carefully invert tin over
tea towel. Your greeting card is ready to

decorate. Do not mar the surface to be
decorated with your fingerprints.

Step 6: Use the writing tip for personal
messages, and the star, flower, and leaf tips
for decorating.

Christmas:

This season is built squarely on four
foundations of happiness: love, children, the
color of the forest, and the making of candies.
Your friends and family will think you've
surpassed yourself in the art of delectable gift
giving when you present them with a grand
selection of sweets from your own kitchen.

Even people who, eleven months of the
year, consider the word "candy" to mean the
wicked, wonderful world of self-indulgence
are drawn into the kitchen to make a batch
or two for Christmas. The following is a
selection of confections that can be prepared
two to three weeks in advance. Make one or
two batches each day and the amount will
grow into a generous assortment to be gift
packaged or dipped in Chocolate, Summer,
Bonbon, or Caramel Coating. Coated candies
will be at their flavor best if dipped just a few
days before they are to be packaged.

Recommended: *(See index for recipes.)*

Fondant
Marzipan
Fudge
Nougat

Brittle
Toffee
Butter Crunch
Divinity
Mints
Candy Canes
Marshmallows
Caramels
Hard Clear Candies
Popcorn Confections
Dried-Fruit Confections

Chanukah:

This Jewish holiday is also known as "The Feast of Lights." Remember the joyous occasion with gold- and silver-decorated boxes of *Sandra's "Noent"* (p. 109).

Valentine's Day:

This is the day when the heart has its reason for giving a large molded chocolate heart decorated with a tender message of love.

Words like "honey" and "sweetheart" go back to the ancient belief in the aphrodisiac quality of quick-energy sweetmeats. The Chinese used honey in sexually stimulating pills and foods. The Arab chiefs painted their harem girls with it. A molded chocolate heart would have met with the approval of the Aztecs, who toasted their love goddess, Xochiquetral, with chocolate. From there, it traveled to the Spanish and French courts, where it became a sensation and was denounced by the clergy as being "immoral."

Metal heart-shaped molds can be obtained from gourmet stores handling utensils. Even a small heart-shaped cake pan can be used. For method refer to instructions for molding greeting cards at the beginning of this section. A beautiful heart can also be molded of Summer Coating. Unmold the heart onto a large heart-shaped paper lace doily.

Lincoln's Birthday:

Observe the simplicity and homespun charm of this day with a gift of old-fashioned candies.

Recommended: *(See index for recipes.)*

Maple Cream Candy
Old-Fashioned Penuche
Black Walnut Pralines
Buttermilk Fudge
Pulled Cream Candy
Kentucky Lemon Brittle

Washington's Birthday:

Legend says George chopped down the cherry tree and ever since cherries and hatchets have been symbols of his birthday.

Recommended: *(See index for recipes.)*

Fondant Mints—decorated with cherries and hatchets
Easy-Do Chocolate-Covered Cherries
Cherry Cordials
Cherry Fudge

St. Patrick's Day:

All hats off to Erin. Give an assortment of *Irish Butterscotch* (p. 110) and light green lime-flavored divinity or marshmallows. For a spunky accent decorate container with green paper derby hats.

Easter:

Effort notwithstanding, Easter is unrivaled in its number of traditional gift-giving confections, from the smallest egg to the largest molded bunny nesting among a handsome arrangement of hand-decorated eggs.

Molded or coated eggs, bunnies, and chicks may be made in the home candy kitchen. See Chapter 20 (pp. 165&171), for coating and molding. In this section you will find illustrations for decorating Easter candies. Very elegant eggs are decorated with candied mint leaves, violets, and rose petals. These can be held in place with a dab of frosting.

Recommended Centers: *(See index for recipes.)*

Fondant
Marzipan
Fudge
Divinity
Marshmallows

Have you ever wondered why eggs, chickens, and bunnies are symbolic of Easter? In the Northern Hemisphere, Easter coincides with spring—a season of new life and renewal of nature. Christianity applied these ancient signs of rebirth to the resurrection of Jesus Christ. The hatching of a baby chicken, which had been entombed in the egg, was considered to represent His rising up out of the grave. The bunny, for obvious reasons, is considered a symbol of fertility and abundance of life.

The tradition of decorating eggs apparently had its origin in a legend concerning Simon Cyrene (one of the men who was at the crucifixion), whose profession was that of an egg merchant. Upon his return from Calvary to his basket of produce (which he had left at the side of the road), he found that one of the eggs was miraculously colored pink and decorated with a purple cross and white tulips. Easter eggs decorated in this tradition are called "Alleluia Eggs," stemming from the Christian expression of thanksgiving.

The Easter Egg Hunt: This is a tradition in America with the bunny bringing eggs to the little children. You may set the stage by hand-decorating your own eggs and hiding them. Invite the children and give each a little basket. Plan prizes for the one who gathers the largest number and for the child who finds the "Alleluia Egg."

Creative Easter-Candy Arrangements:
Anyone should be pleased to receive the usual woven reed basket lined with cellophane grass and filled with delicious home-made confections. However, with little effort and expense, the traditional candies can be presented in recycled containers—pretty enough to capture the imagination of anyone. The following are ideas I have used with great success:

Plastic Berry Baskets: For these I like to weave pastel ribbons through the open slots and attach to each a braided handle stiffened with a length of florist's wire. Ribbon bows or paper flowers can be used to hide the spot where the handle is attached.

Styrofoam Egg Cartons: These come in white or soft pastels. At Eastertime Blum's of San Francisco sell their expensive coated eggs packaged in these cartons, which are prominently displayed in the best department stores around the country. Save your own cartons and line them with cellophane grass to cushion the eggs. Any outside printing can be covered with paper cutouts or decals. These make ideal containers for packing and shipping.

One-, Two-, and Three-Pound Ham Cans: Look for the Armour can or any other with a flip-top and save the plastic cover. Look again and you will really be seeing a large egg. Pleat and fold a generous width of pastel nylon net around the can and tie a large bow at the top. Line the can with cellophane grass and fill with an Easter Candy assortment. Use the plastic cover if the candies are to be packaged and shipped.

Deviled-Egg Plate: Most of us have one of these around. Use this container to arrange an intriguing edible centerpiece. Make the center the bunny's nest and place hand-decorated eggs in the indented impressions.

Passover:

This is a Jewish festival beginning on the fourteenth of Nisan and traditionally celebrated for eight days. Hand-dipped chocolate, chocolate-covered matzos, or matzos covered with Summer Coating would be appropriate for this occasion.

May Baskets:

Remember these from your grade-school days when you spent the early spring days making square and cone-shaped baskets, using construction paper, scissors, paste, crepe paper, and leftover Christmas ribbon? These would be filled to overflowing with an abundance of fragrant flowers, gathered from gardens or nearby woods. Tucked down under all the floral splendor would be a bag of candies, which the community mothers had prepared the day before. Hard candies were much favored because they could be individually wrapped to withstand the frequent handling by little hands.

Recommended: *(See index for recipes.)*

Toffee
Brittle
Butter Crunch

Mother's Day:

The same molded heart you used for Valentine's Day can be used for Mother's Day. Almost any candy is suitable, but make sure it is candy that mother likes.

Recommended: *(See index for recipes.)*

Candies with Summer Coating
Hand-dipped Bonbons, decorated with candied leaves and flowers
Pink and White Marshmallows
Pink Coconut Fudge

Father's Day:

Give father a molded chocolate greeting card—he's still a little boy at heart—and convey your message of love with frosting tubes.

July Fourth:

It's picnic, boating, and camping time. Take along individually wrapped bags of *Old-Fashioned Molasses-Peanut Popcorn* (p. 144) tied with red, white, and blue ribbon.

Halloween:

Have ready for the cute little trick-or-treat goblins at your door a selection of homemade confections in the traditional colors—red, orange, and black: red for fire, always feared by the witches; orange for the golden harvest; and black for demons.

Recommended: *(See index for recipes.)*

Red Taffy Apples
Orange Lollipops
Mr. Owl and Miss Pussy Cat Popcorn
    Confections
Chocolate Coated Pretzels

Thanksgiving:

This is probably the richest holiday of all because it signifies the end of the harvest season. Grace the Thanksgiving table with a selection of appropriate confections.

Recommended: *(See index for recipes.)*

Mints
Candied Nuts
Glazed Dried Fruits
Molded Marzipan Fruits

How to Gift Wrap Containers

During any season, a gift of candy made in your own kitchen is welcome to almost everyone. An assortment of hand-dipped chocolates and other confections expresses your thoughtfulness with the unspoken message, "I cared enough to make this just for you."

Only the very finest and most expensive confectioners hand-decorate their candy boxes. Your offerings will become more personal, more appealing, and prettier, done up in festive wrappings or tucked into a useful container that is part of the giving. Packaged attractively, they become a present you'll be doubly proud to give.

Even if you are just slightly artistic, you might want to give some thought to making and decorating your own containers. Once you have adopted the habit of searching for clever containers, you'll notice all sorts of objects to use for packaging your candies. Thrift and secondhand stores, auctions, and garage sales will turn up canisters, wooden bowls, large seashells, old Mason jars, small flower pots, et cetera. Gift shops usually carry a wide variety of party-type boxes and unusual paper containers.

For a start, look for inexpensive apothecary jars. Fill them with a colorful assortment of uncoated candies and tie with a bright bow and a romantic fake nosegay. I prefer to use one- and two-pound coffee tins after they have been thoroughly washed and aired to remove the slightest hint of a coffee scent. They also make ideal airtight containers for storing and shipping. Cover them with decorative adhesive-backed paper or use

Elmer's glue to cover them with gift-wrap paper. These also look very attractive covered with felt or fabric and decorated with gold paper doilies, gold braid, and ribbons. Paper cutouts offer another inexpensive way to decorate canisters and boxes.

Tops of coffee cans and boxes can be covered with a ribbon cluster to form a pompom. You can also create a confetti effect by using contrasting colors.

Even though they are frankly fake, paper flowers can be used to good advantage in covering canisters and boxes. Making the flowers is a good rainy-day project for the whole family.

Today, you can find gift-wrap papers in a more fascinating selection than ever before, with hundreds of designs and something for every occasion. In our family we like to save our single-layer boxes and cover them with a gift-wrapping paper we make with colored tissue paper pressed over foil. This gives an expensive-looking custom-made finish to any candy container. If you have plenty of time and want to give your candy gifts a personally designed touch, you might like to go a bit arty and create a simple collage by pasting patterns over the tissue-foil paper.

Plumbridge in New York is an old and elegant sweetmeat shop in the fashionable East Sixties. Here a customer will find a copy of the *Social Register* discreetly reposing on a small table beside a selection of gift cards, pens, and ink. In this store a customer is likely to find an ordinary berry basket from the supermarket lined with a white lace paper doily and serving as a container to hold a clear plastic bag of candies tied at the top with a bright ribbon. Berry baskets can also be made attractive by running ribbon in and out of the open slots to create a basket-weave appearance.

How To Make Your Own Gift Wrap:

I recommend using a white glue such as Elmer's, which dries clear.

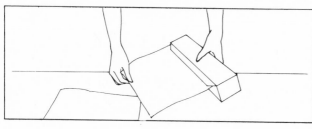

Step 1: Measure off a length of aluminum foil about 12 inches long or enough to cover container to be used. Also cut a sheet of colored tissue paper the same size.

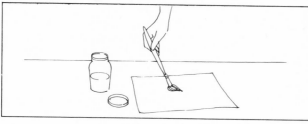

Step 2: Place aluminum foil on table, shiny side up. Coat the entire surface with a mixture of half glue and half water, using a soft brush. (It is very easy to measure the glue and water in a small jar and then shake to blend.)

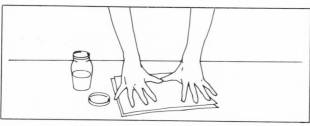

Step 3: Place colored tissue paper over the glued surface of the aluminum foil. Both pastel and brilliant colors work very well. Carefully smooth the tissue paper. There will be some wrinkling but this merely adds to the final effect.

Step 4: Brush glue mixture over the tissue paper. Do not be alarmed if the paper tears slightly. After the paper is pressed the foil shining through will be very attractive. Let dry at least one hour.

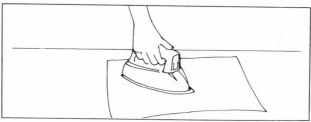

Step 5: Place two sheets of waxed paper over the foil paper and cover with brown wrapping paper to keep the iron from sticking to the waxed paper. Press at steam setting. Strip away the brown and waxed paper, and the tissue paper and foil will be welded together.

How to Cover Cans and Boxes:

To Cover a Can:

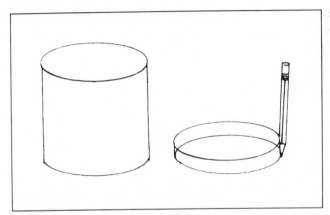

Step 1: Trace the top and bottom of the can (or cylinder) and cut two circles.

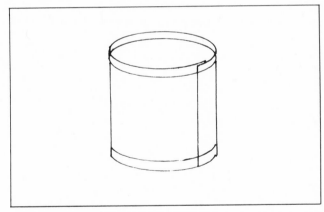

Step 2: Wrap the can, trimming the overlap so it can be turned under slightly. Secure with glue or concealed tape. The paper should extend over top and bottom of the can slightly.

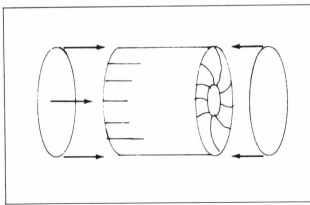

Step 3: Snip the edges of the wrapping paper even with the edges of the can. Secure with glue or tape by turning under. Attach the circles to the top and bottom with glue or concealed tape.

Variations:

Cover lid with doily and weave a ribbon through the edges.

Greeting cards make lovely decorations for cans over plain colored wrapping paper. Make a pom-pom for the top of the can (see p. 208).

To Cover Boxes:

The flat box with a cover-all lid is the best type to use. This eliminates the trouble of covering the bottom half.

Before cutting expensive paper or fabric, first practice with brown wrapping paper. This way you can fit and measure a pattern for the final cutting.

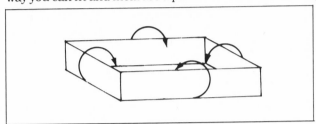

Step 1: For the lid, measure from the inside edge of each side to the opposite inside edge, allowing for a fold over of at least ½ inch at sides and ends of the lid.

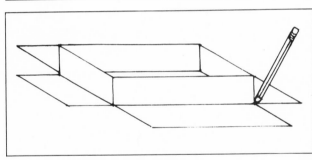

Step 2: Mark the measurements off on wrong side of paper with light pencil marks and cut paper to size. Place the box lid upside down in the center and trace around it.

I do not recommend applying the glue directly onto the covering. This causes paper to tear easily and makes fabrics stretch.

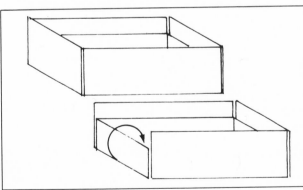

Step 3: Use a glue stick or soft brush dipped in glue to lightly cover box lid and sides. Turn the lid upside down on the marked paper. Turn over and carefully smooth out wrinkles. Then turn the paper down around the sides of the box lid. Trim folds at corners or turn in and glue the flaps lightly against side of box. Turn the fold over inside the box lid. Secure with glue or concealed tape.

Step 4: Attach ribbon to inside of box lid with glue. Decorate top of lid with ribbon bow or flower.

How to Make Ribbon Pompom:

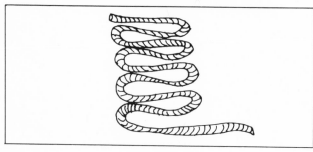

Step 1: Loop the ribbon or yarn back and forth until desired number of loops is reached. Two colors may be used, looped together.

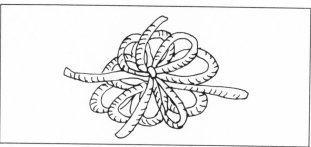

Step 2: Tie very tightly in center with separate piece of ribbon or yarn to form the pompom.

Step 3: If using yarn, tie knots at loose ends.

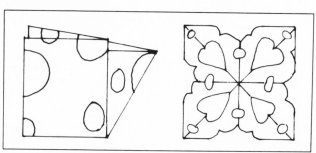

How to Use Paper-Cutouts for Decorating:

This is the craft we learned in grade school. Simply fold squares of white or colored paper into sixths—snip, cut, and unfold a magical transformation to glue over a can or box covered with your own handmade gift wrap.

How to Make Paper Flowers:

The following three easy examples are recommended for the beginner:

Materials:

Colored tissue or art paper
Pipe stems or florist wire (I dip pipe stems in a strong
    solution of green food coloring and water.)
Plastic or fabric leaves (optional)

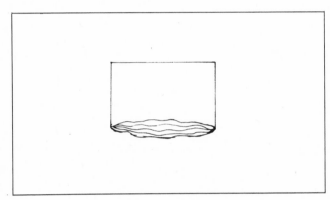

Step 1: Measure off a length of tissue paper 20 inches long and 4 inches wide. Fold in half lengthwise to make a strip 20 inches long and 2 inches wide. Fold this strip three times to make a square 2¼ inches x 2 inches.

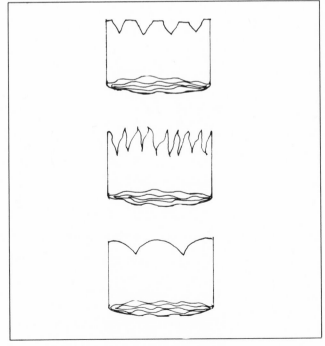

Step 2: Cut any of these designs.

Carnation: Use pinking shears to cut top edge. Cut apart at folds.

Petal Flower: Cut apart at folds.

Rose: Cut apart at folds.

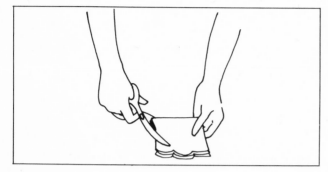

Step 3: Cut along the folds of each flower and you will have sixteen pieces to twist around the stem to make a small flower.

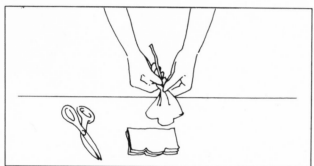

Step 4: Hold the stem in the left hand and start pinch-pleating the pieces of tissue tightly around the stem. Use gummed tape to hold tissue to stem.

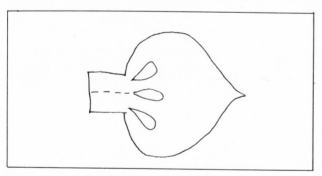

Step 5: Attach purchased leaves or make your own.

Step 6: Pinch-pleat lower end of leaf around stem of flower and secure with tape.

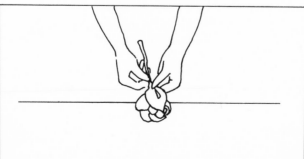

Step 7: Tie flowers onto candy container or box with ribbon bow.

How to Make a Christmas Tree:

A very unusual Christmas tree is covered with ribbon loops filled with candy treats to use as a centerpiece or for gift giving.

Materials:

9-inch Styrofoam cone
Florist's wire picks (available at florist shops), or short
    hairpins
10 yards green fabric ribbon (velvet, satin, or gingham), 2
    inches wide, or cut your own strips from fabric and
    use pinking shears to finish edges
5 yards red yarn or ribbon, ¼-inch wide

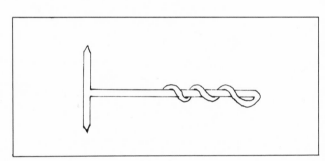

Step 1: Bend florist's picks in half and rewind wire around short pointed half.

Step 2: Measure and cut green ribbons into 6-inch lengths. Fold each length in half and make loop. You will need about 50 loops.

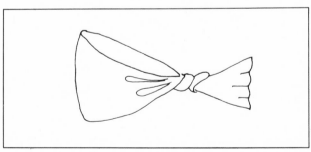

Step 3: Attach to pick, twisting wire around securely.

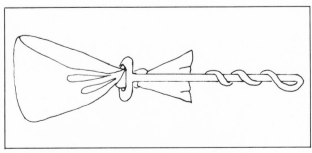

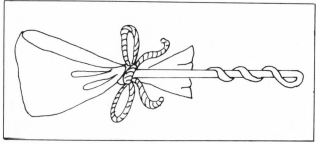

Step 4: Tie on yarn bows for a finished look.

Step 5: Working around base of cone, push in a row of ribbon loops, side by side. Repeat next row. Continue this procedure up to the top of the cone.

Step 6: Fill loops with hand-dipped candies or other confections. Tree can be reused.

Storing and Freezing Candy and Confections

Homemade candy keeps well for two or three weeks if properly stored in airtight containers in a cool, dry place at about 65°F. or 18°C. Candy can be made ahead of time; in fact, some types need a day or two to ripen, or mature, to their best flavors. Still, it is well to keep in mind that freshness is one of the reasons most people enjoy homemade candy and confections.

Candies are generally divided into two categories: the creamy confections and the brittle, crackly, crystalline ones. Do not store hard candies in the same container with soft, creamy candies because the moisture from the softer candy may make the hard candies sticky.

Wrap all caramel, taffy, and nougat before storing to prevent spreading. Keep chocolate and other hand-dipped candies in crinkle cups, or use some other means of keeping them from touching each other, and store in single layers (I recycle my plastic meat trays) until time to arrange gift-box assortments. Never pile coated candies in plastic bags because this will mar the desired gloss of the finished product. Hand-dipped candies are rather delicate in comparison to the commercially made products which usually contain paraffin and preservatives to give them good shipping qualities.

All candies will keep almost indefinitely if properly wrapped in airtight freezer bags or containers.

Popcorn balls can also be frozen. Wrap each in individual freezer bag.

Most dried fruit confections can also be wrapped and frozen.

Candies may be dipped in coating and gift-boxed before being frozen. Just remember to double bag the box to eliminate the slightest possibility of an air leak.

How to Remove Candies from Freezer:

Remove and let stand several hours to warm to room temperature before opening containers or bags. This prevents moisture from collecting on candies due to change in temperature. *Caution:* This is particularly important if the candies are to be dipped in Chocolate Coating. If the candies have already been coated with chocolate, they should never be taken out of the freezer container or bag until they have thawed completely. Removing them too soon will cause gray streaks to form on the coating from the sudden temperature change.

How to Box Candies

Boxes for finished candies can be purchased from confectioners' supply houses and some paper supply stores such as Hallmark and Dennison. There are two popular types—the folding and the single-layer box. The latter is far the best and most professional-looking if making candies for profit. Any single-layer box can be covered.

How to Prepare Box:

Candy-box dividers, liner padding, and crinkle cups can be ordered from confectioners' supply houses. (See Sources of Supply, p. 217.) However, for the casual candy cook who only occasionally wants to give a gift of candy, waxed paper or paper lace doilies can be used for the lining. You can also make your own dividers or crinkle cups.

Either will keep the candies from slipping around in the box and protect them from rubbing against each other.

If using waxed paper to line the box, cut the waxed paper three times the length and three times the width of the box to be packed. This will take two strips of paper, one to fold over the other. Paper lace doilies should have an overhang of at least 4 inches on all sides.

Examples:
Cutting the paper to line box.

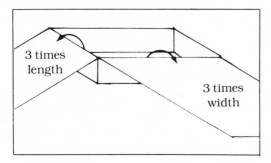

Cutting Dividers.

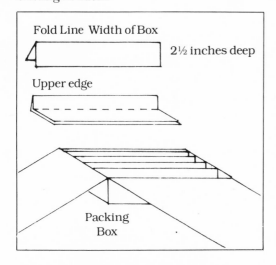

To make cardboard dividers cut light-weight white cardboard 2½ inches wide and the width of the box. Fold this strip in half lengthwise and crease in half lengthwise.

Crease lower edge ⅓ again so the folded edge is uppermost and lower edge is bent to go under a row of candies. The number of dividers needed depends on the size of the box. Eight dividers should be sufficient to package one pound of candies.

An alternative to making dividers is making your own crinkle cups from heavy-duty foil. (See illustrations.) These are made by cutting a square of foil 5 x 5 inches. You may cut several squares at one time, but you must be exact in the cutting. Crease each piece of foil in quarters to determine the center of the square. Unfold and turn each corner into the center of the square. Again, turn the corners in. Reverse the square and once more turn the corners to the center. Reverse the square. In this position place the left thumb in the center of the square. With the right thumb and index finger pull up the top four corners to resemble a tulip. You will have four square corners on the bottom. Tuck these under to reinforce the bottom of the cup and you will have a perfect little foil flower to hold a candy center.

How to Fill Candy Box:

Use the left hand and quickly place candy in cup. Remember to hold dipped candy with a very light touch so glossy finish is not marred by fingerprints. You might want to wear white cotton gloves if the kitchen is warm. If using dividers, pack one row of candies, then insert a divider, pushing the standing-up portion firmly against the row. Continue until the box appears full. You should be able to insert one more row by holding the last divider firmly in place and tight against the last row of candies you have placed in the box. It is wise to pack firmly if the candies are for sale or are to be wrapped for mailing. Empty spaces in the box may be filled with coated nut meats or other small confections. Never put in the box anything that is not edible.

How to Make Crinkle Cups with Foil:

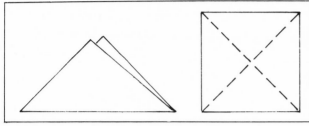

1. Cut heavy-duty foil in 5-inch square and fold to determine center point—unfold.

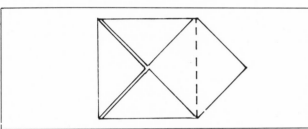

2. Turn four corners to center.

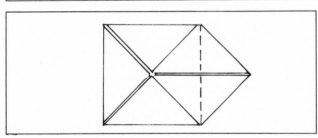

3. Again turn four corners to center.

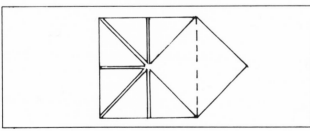

4. Reverse and turn four corners to center.

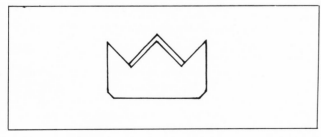

5. Reverse again. In this position place the left thumb in the center of the square and hold. With the right thumb and index finger pull up the top four corners to resemble a tulip. Tuck the four corners under to round the bottom of the cup.

How to Mail Candy

The following suggestions are recommended for sending candies and confections by mail:

1. Send candy and confections that will stay fresh for a long time.

Recommended: *(See index for recipes.)*

Cooked and Uncooked Fondants
Dried-Fruit Confections
Nougat
Butter Crunch
Caramels
Marzipan
Fudge
Toffee
Marshmallows

2. Do not send candy that will soften or become soggy in warm, humid climates.

Not Recommended:

Divinity
Brittle
Jellies
Coated Fresh Fruit
Taffy
Hard Clear Candies
Creole Pralines
Coated Pretzels

3. Do not mail hand-dipped chocolates between the months May through October.

4. Use a good, durable container. A metal box or canister is best for mailing.

5. Wrap each kind of candy separately in foil or plastic so flavors won't mingle.

6. Pack candy tightly. Do not use popcorn for extra packing inside the container because this taste will be absorbed into the porous candy.

7. Seal candy container in airtight plastic bag and then cushion it in larger container or box with Styrofoam packing curliques. Pack tightly to withstand the tossing and handling received enroute to destination.

8. Print name and address outside of box, then wrap candy securely. Print name and address on label and place on top side of package only.

9. Write or have post office stamp "perishable" on package. Special handling is available for a small extra fee, or send air mail for about the same cost.

10. Mail overseas holiday packages early and the fastest way possible. Check with your post office for this information.

Sources of Supply

If your time is limited for shopping, or if you live far out on the rural route, the following companies will supply high-quality candy-making equipment and ingredients. There is an initial charge of $1.00 for the Maid of Scandinavia catalog, and the cost of the Wilton Yearbook is $2.50. Other listed sources supply complimentary brochures and catalogs.

Almond Paste

Maid of Scandinavia
3244 Raleigh Avenue
Minneapolis, Minn. 55416

Candy Box Liners and Padding
Candy Boxes

Maid of Scandinavia
3244 Raleigh Avenue
Minneapolis, Minn. 55416

Candy Thermometer

Maid of Scandinavia
3244 Raleigh Avenue
Minneapolis, Minn. 55416

Kitchen Glamor Inc.
26770 Grand River
Detroit, Mich. 48240

Carob Powder

Maid of Scandinavia
3244 Raleigh Avenue
Minneapolis, Minn. 55416

Crinkle Cups for Candies

Maid of Scandinavia
3244 Raleigh Avenue
Minneapolis, Minn. 55416

Wilton Enterprises, Inc.
833 West 115th Street
Chicago, Ill. 60643

Kitchen Glamor Inc.
26770 Grand River
Detroit, Mich. 48240

Cutting Wheel
(Use Pizza Cutter)

Maid of Scandinavia
3244 Raleigh Avenue
Minneapolis, Minn. 55416

Dipping Fork

Maid of Scandinavia
3244 Raleigh Avenue
Minneapolis, Minn. 55416

Flavoring Extracts and Oils

Maid of Scandinavia
3244 Raleigh Avenue
Minneapolis, Minn. 55416

Wilton Enterprises, Inc.
833 West 115th Street
Chicago, Ill. 60643

Kitchen Glamor Inc.
26770 Grand River
Detroit, Mich. 48240

Fondant Paddle

Maid of Scandinavia
3244 Raleigh Avenue
Minneapolis, Minn. 55416

Food Colors
(Paste and Liquid)

Maid of Scandinavia
3244 Raleigh Avenue
Minneapolis, Minn. 55416

Wilton Enterprises, Inc.
833 West 115th Street
Chicago, Ill. 60643

Kitchen Glamor Inc.
26770 Grand River
Detroit, Mich. 48240

Funnel and Stick

Maid of Scandinavia
3244 Raleigh Avenue
Minneapolis, Minn. 55416

Wilton Enterprises, Inc.
833 West 115th Street
Chicago, Ill. 60643

Marzipan Stems and Leaves

Maid of Scandinavia
3244 Raleigh Avenue
Minneapolis, Minn. 55416

Wilton Enterprises, Inc.
833 West 115th Street
Chicago, Ill. 60643

Kitchen Glamor Inc.
26770 Grand River
Detroit, Mich. 48240

Molds and Forms

Maid of Scandinavia
3244 Raleigh Avenue
Minneapolis, Minn. 55416

Kitchen Glamor Inc.
26770 Grand River
Detroit, Mich. 48240

Wilton Enterprises, Inc.
833 West 115th Street
Chicago, Ill. 60643

Professional Dipping Chocolate

Maid of Scandinavia
3244 Raleigh Avenue
Minneapolis, Minn. 55416

Bissinger's
205 West Fourth Street
Cincinnati, Ohio 45202

Kitchen Glamor Inc.
26770 Grand River
Detroit, Mich. 48240

White Coating

Maid of Scandinavia
3244 Raleigh Avenue
Minneapolis, Minn. 55416

Kitchen Glamor Inc.
26770 Grand River
Detroit, Mich. 48240

Index